John Keith Edington

1007 CEO's CONFIRM
EVERYTHING YOU NEED TO LEARN ABOUT LEADERSHIP
YOU CAN LEARN FROM A P1NEAPPLE

Copyright 2014 by John Keith Edington;

All Rights Reserved.

ISBN: 978-1-291-76828-2

Published by:

Court yard Publications
The Old School
Constable Burton
Leyburn, North Yorkshire

No part of this work may be reproduced or stored in any information retrieval system without the express permission of the publisher is in writing.

John Keith Edington author of:

- *Great leaders never climb smooth mountains: how to avoid the 17 1/2 routes to ineffective leadership*

- *You cannot lead the cavalry charge if you think you look silly on a horse: developing a leadership mind-set*

- *People know what to do so why the hell don't they do it?*

1007 CEO's CONFIRM

EVERYTHING YOU NEED TO LEARN ABOUT LEADERSHIP YOU CAN LEARN FROM A P1NEAPPLE

Discover why collaboration is the number one trait CEO's seek from their managers and leaders

JOHN KEITH EDINGTON

"This fast-moving, practical book is loaded with proven strategies to help you get better results as a manager or leader in any organization."
Brian Tracy – Author, How The Best Leaders Lead

Success stories

❝ *John has given me the power and methodology to logically work through issues swiftly with positive outcomes".* - Dean Jennings: Kongsberg Maritime Sales Manager Off Shore Production Systems UK and Ireland.

❝ *JKE is truly a master in his field and his passion to help you and I succeed leaps off every page. With a prestigious career in personal development, John shares all of the very best nuggets here. It's pure genius to associate the pineapple with leadership, but as John explains it, it makes perfect sense - when you read the book, you'll understand why. I highly recommend you get your own copy and get your hands on a real gem that will open your mind to new ways to achieve even greater success".* - Dawn Grossart FCIM Co-Director of Reality Productions Ltd.

❝ *This fast-moving, practical book is loaded with proven strategies to help you get better results as a manager or leader in any organization."* - Brian Tracy – Author, How The Best Leaders Lead.

❝ *Johns knowledge and wisdom shines through once again, this book is a must for anyone who is looking to enhance their career or to take their business to the next level".* - Simon J Gilbert, Author of How Big is Your But: "Releasing the Mental Handbrake on your Success" - Founder of: The Think and Grow Rich Academy.

❝ *John's book shows a great new twist on leadership and is easy to follow and understand. The acronyms are well laid out and are full of thought provoking questions. The book contains interesting facts and figures and I would recommend it others wanting to get a grip on leadership."* - Richard Penny. MD Oak by Design Harrogate.

Acknowledgements

I would like to thank my clients who have attended my workshops, seminars and those who have been through the leadership mentoring program for sharing their valuable knowledge for us all to learn from.

To Moira, my wife, for her love and support thank you.

Simon Gilbert, Jim Rohn and Zig Ziglar for all your help, guidance and above all, your knowledge; true friends and mentors, thank you.

A special thank you to 3 very talented people:

Danila, for her editing and proofreading.

Please contact her at: http://danilahaddon.elance.com

and

Milos and Biljana for the design of the book cover and bringing the pineapple to life.

Please contact them at: https://www.elance.com/s/onokao1/

And finally my fellow mastermind group members, where our several minds will always prove that the whole is greater than the sum of the parts.

CONTENTS

What Takes A Person From Average to Outstanding 8

What is the psychology of leadership mastery 18

Why did I write the book? 23

Why is self-awareness so vital to our success? 25

Pineapple equals leadership 31

People know what to do so why the hell don't they do it? 43

How to add value 67

Change Management 86

Ebbinghaus Curve 96

Motivation and Momentum 99

The 17 competencies that underpin leadership mastery 106

The six laws of the mind 120

Creating flow and goal achievement 127

Goal setting workbook 131

A final thought 151

What Takes A Person From Average To Outstanding

The book you are now holding in your hand seeks to answer some of the most important and remarkably frustrating questions that many leaders, managers, or supervisors have been asking themselves and of the people that they work with, for generations.

Hello, my name is John Edington, below are the very questions that have been the focus of my twenty-five year research into the psychology of leadership mastery. The questions are:

1. What takes a person from average to outstanding?

2. What are the differences between an outstanding performer and an average one?

3. And more importantly, why if people know what to do, why the hell don't they do it?

I have been studying the difference that makes the difference in a leader, and the mind-sets and behaviour's needed to go from average to outstanding; research which I have compiled into a library of ideas that transform knowledge into positive action when implemented by leaders. In searching for answers to these question and many more on leadership, I have discovered that the pineapple is the perfect metaphor, to help take you from where you are now, in your career, to outstanding.

Let me explain.

Everything You Need To Learn About Leadership You Can Learn From A P1NEAPPLE

Did you know that the pineapple is not a single fruit; it is a corosis. The fruits of a hundred of more separate flowers grow on the pineapple's core. As they grow they swell with juice and pulp, expanding and fusing together to become the rich fruit. As a leader, manager, or supervisor, it is vital that we copy the lessons learned from the pineapple. We need to involve, inspire, and ignite those we manage to come together around the central core of the business. The pineapple is rightly known as the king of fruits, it would not be what it is today, if each flower / employee worked in isolation.

THE PiNEAPPLE MAN

Leadership Insights From 1007 C.E.O.'s

A fascinating survey of one thousand and seven CEOs found that collaboration is the number one trait they seek in their employees, with seventy-five percent of CEOs calling it critical.

The definition of collaboration is your ability to get every department/ person, to be just like the pineapple; to come together around the central core of the business.

Collaboration is the difference between people getting from the day, not just through the day. It is connecting to the positive experience of being part of the team.

Quite simply put, a picture of a car will never be the same as actually driving it or a picture of the beach is never the same as feeling the sand between your toes, or the coolness of the ocean. Getting from the day is far more rewarding, then getting through the day. The research findings also identified that, leaders are recognising that our new connected era, is fundamentally changing how people engage. This shift is one reason why it is vital for today's leaders to think and more importantly, to act like pineapples.

In a results driven world, more and more people feel that they are just a cog in a machine. The problem this creates is that talented people don't go to work just to complete tasks, they want to offer ideas that can be discussed freely, honestly and respectfully. They not only want to grow professionally, they want to feel that they contribute to the future success of the company. They want to be able to adapt to the present and to shape the future; faster, easier, and better than their competitors. They want to get from the day, not just through the day.

The following quote sums up collaboration:

"You can design the most wonderful business in the world, but it takes people to make your dream a reality".

We know that getting the best out of people is more rewarding, than constantly trying to get the most out of them. Your task, as a leader has to be concerned with how we get the best from those we manage because I have found that people who give their best, automatically give their most.

Leadership is helping people to give their best every time.

My definition of leadership is this; the transferring of both ideas and a positive vision of a desired outcome from one mind to others.

How well you transfer your ideas and positive vision will determine the success you achieve in life, your career, and business.

This is the starting point of our journey together. To study the difference that makes the difference in helping you become a leadership master. Wouldn't it make perfect sense, that if you want to be wealthy, you would study wealth, and if you wanted to be happy, then you would study happiness? If you want to be successful in life and your career, then study the lessons learned from the pineapple; that of getting the best out of every individual including ourselves.

Let's begin our journey, by taking guidance and wisdom from Maya Angelu:

"People may not remember everything you did, or everything you said, but they will always remember how you made them feel".

How you make people feel will determine your success as a manager or leader. The successful transfer of ideas from one mind to another is totally dependent on how you made them feel. Was it involved, inspired and ignited or did you leave them feeling rebuffed, rejected and resentful?

People often say that what you don't know won't hurt you. A recent survey of over forty-one thousand successful managers revealed, that the exact opposite is true. Organisations benefit more from leaders who take responsibility for what they don't know, rather than leaders who pretend to know it all.

Self-awareness is probably one of the least discussed leadership competencies, and yet it is one of the most valuable.

Self-awareness is being conscience of what you're good at, while acknowledging what you still have yet to learn.

This includes admitting when you don't have the answers and owning up to mistakes.

In our highly competitive culture, this can seem counter intuitive. In fact, many people operate on the belief that they must appear as though they know everything, all of the time, or else people will question their ability, diminishing their effectiveness as a leader. And yet if we were to be totally honest with ourselves, you would admit really, that the opposite is true.

Because; whether you acknowledge your weakness or not, everyone still sees them. So rather than conceal them, the person who tries to hide weaknesses, actually highlights them, creating the perception of a lack of integrity. As the lack of integrity grows, so does the lack of trust and once a lack of trust has been established, the levels of creativity and output will diminish.

The benefits of self-awareness in relation to collaboration

It is easy to see how pretending to know everything when you don't can create problematic situations for your entire organisation.

On the other hand, when you take responsibility for what you don't know, you, your organisation, and the people that look up to you for leadership, all benefit. On an interpersonal level, being self-aware of your strengths and weaknesses will earn the trust of others and increase your credibility. Both of which will increase your leadership effectiveness.

On an organisational level, the benefits are even greater. When you acknowledge what you have yet to learn, you're modelling in your organisation that it's ok to admit you don't have all the answers, to make mistakes, but more importantly, to ask for help. These are all characteristics of an organisation that is consistently learning, and springboards to innovation and growth, two hallmarks of high performing organisations.

Take a minute to reflect on what are your signature strengths as a manager or leader? List at least 3:

1. _____.
2. _____.
3. _____.
4. _____.
5. _____.

What is the number one area you feel as a manager or leader that you need to strengthen?

- _____.

The following piece of poetry sums up brilliantly the fear and insecurity that people who pretend to know everything self-generate.

There is Something I Don't Know

There is something I don't know
that I am supposed to know.
I don't know what it is I don't know,
and yet I am supposed to know,

I feel I look stupid
if I appear not to know what it is I don't know
therefore, I pretend I know.
This is nerve-wracking since I don't know
therefore I must continually pretend to know everything.

I feel you know what I am supposed to know
but you can't tell me what it is, because
you really don't know that I don't know what it is

My real frustration is that; you may know what I don't know,
but I can't ask you to help me with what I don't know
So please assume I don't know and tell me everything.

John Edington
Edited from R. D. Lang in Knots

> **If you lack self-awareness you can't change. Why should you? As far as you're concerned you're doing everything right.**
> ~ Jim Whitt

> " Awareness is like the sun. When it shines on things, they are transformed. "
> ~ Thich Nhat Hanh ~

There are five major areas that managers, leaders and supervisors will benefit from reading this book or joining The Psychology of Leadership Mastery Mentoring Program.

1. To become the person that company's fight to keep: You have invested a lot of time, effort, and money into your career so far, in this uncertain economic time. *"Everything you ever needed to learn about leadership you can learn from a pineapple!"* will help you get the best return on your investment in you. Getting the best is far more rewarding than getting the most out of people.

2. Establishing a rewarding career does not always mean a higher salary, it may mean you acquire the prestige, status, and influence that will carry you through all areas of your life.

3. Become the person people look up to, no matter how tall they grow! Learn how to form and maintain lasting relationships in work and in your personal life that are built on Trust and Respect.

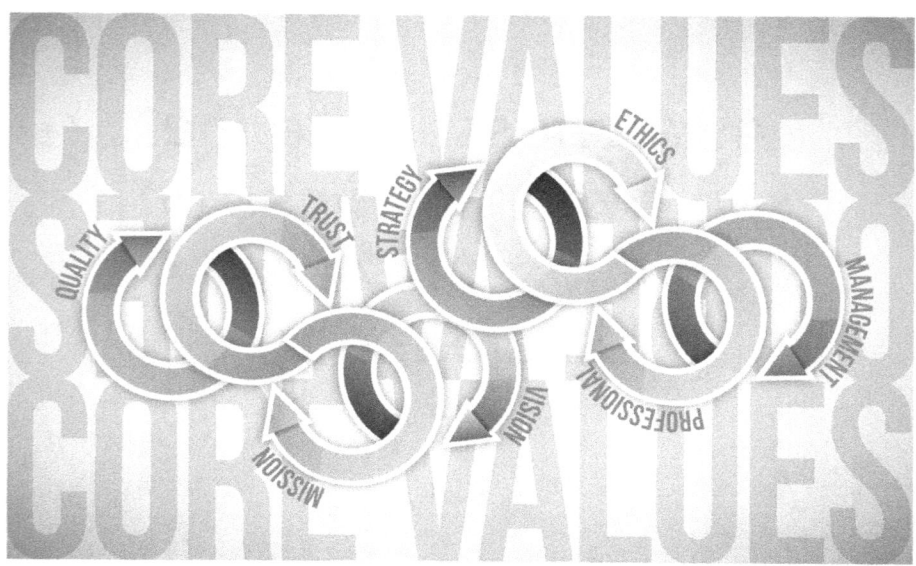

4. Become the best you can be and be the master of your own destiny. Experience the challenge of opening up new areas of your life and feel the excitement of practicing new skills that will help you get the best out of life.

5. All human beings have a built in desire to be emotionally connected with life. We need to feel alive and have meaning and purpose in our lives. We do not have time for boredom and mindless repetition.

From the above five benefits which of them do you resonate with?

If you now look back at your answers on page 11; how do they relate to your signature strengths?

John Keith Edington

What is The Psychology of Leadership Mastery?

Psychology is defined as the study of mind and behaviour.

Helping people to achieve their goals in life, be that career or personal goals, has been my passion for over 25 years. Once I had discovered that, "its knowing how to be different that makes the difference", my life has never been the same.

Leadership is defined as: the transferring of ideas to the minds of others. As a leader, your success will be determined by your ability to transfer your ideas into the minds of those you manage and lead.

In writing this book: ***Everything You Need To Learn About Leadership You Can Learn From A Pineapple;*** I wanted to share with you the "why to" and "how to" learn the lessons offered by the pineapple. As a leader, manager, or supervisor, it is vital that we copy the lessons learned from the pineapple. We need to involve, inspire, and ignite, those we manage, to come together around the central core of the business. The pineapple would not be what it is today, if each flower worked in isolation.

Mastery is a journey that enables us to be better today than we were yesterday'.

Photo taken by proud dad, Jamie Logan of his son Dexter.

If we and the people we manage are better every day than we were yesterday, all our lives and careers would be greatly enhanced.

Mastery is a journey, not a destination.

The Psychology of Leadership Mastery Program is dedicated to transforming knowledge into positive action, by sharing the tools and techniques that allow us to know how to be different and to be better today than yesterday.

I have put together a library of ideas of how to go from where you are now to the person company's fight to keep. As a leader, manager or supervisor the most productive way to build a team that works together, is to genuinely want to help people be the best 'they' can be.

You can have everything in life you want, if you will just help other people get what they want. -Zig Ziglar.

I can guarantee you that people who give their best will automatically give their most compared to people who are forced to give their most, they will inevitably either quit and leave or, more worryingly, they quit and stay.

Quit and stay means, they turn up each day and do as little as possible for the same pay as those who are giving their best. How many people have you worked with who have quit and stayed?

If your job was to fly to the moon and you were 1° off course, when the time had come to arrive on the surface of the moon you would realize that you had missed the moon by four thousand one hundred and sixty-two miles, simply by not correcting your course just 1°!

Leadership is not all about the big decisions, and making grand changes, as you have seen one degree can make a massive difference.

This book is a collection of tried, tested and proven little changes you can make to improve your ability to transfer your ideas into the minds of those you manage.

The Dalai Lama certainly does come out with some fantastic quotes and I love it when he follows what he is saying with his cheeky little chuckle. This one is one of my personal favourites:

If you think little things don't make a difference, try sleeping with a mosquito in the bedroom!

Better still lets learn from Gold medal winner Lizzy Yarnold. Lizzy won gold in the 2014 winter Olympics in Sochi by hurtling down the ice on a tray at 80 kilometres per hour.

Her four runs were faster than her competitors, her first three runs were smoother and with less bumping on the bends than on her forth.

When Lizzy was interviewed a few days after receiving her gold medal she was asked about the fourth run not being as good as the first three; her response was totally inspiring and a great lesson in leadership mastery.

She said:

"You have to remember that no run is ever perfect the trick is to get back on track quicker and faster that everyone else."

The Pineapple metaphor and The Psychology of Leadership Mastery Program is all about helping you, and those you lead, not only get back on track quicker and faster than everyone else but to stay on track as near to perfect as possible all of the time.

Everything You Need To Learn About Leadership You Can Learn From A P1NEAPPLE

John Keith Edington

Who hasn't needed a helping hand now and again?

Recently, I had the great pleasure of attending my niece's third birthday party, at a local child friendly pub. In the manner of any confident three year old, who knows exactly what she wants, Bella ordered me to take her to play with the toys!

While she was playing, I managed to park myself on a window ledge to enjoy watching the collection of children playing. At that point, a little boy wobbled around the large plastic Wendy house. This little man was only just walking; his balance seemed to be tested with every step that he took, until he decided to climb up the slide that was designed for exiting not entering the Wendy house....

After several failed attempts of climbing up, and instantly sliding back down again, from my vantage point on the window ledge, I held out my hand and placed it under his little right foot. This was the leverage he had been searching for; he was now climbing to the top. He knew nothing of my helping hand; he was unaware of the part I had played in his success. He was equally unaware of the part he had played, in reminding me why I loved the psychology of achievement so much.

We all have benefited at some point in our lives from a helping hand, a kind word, a new sense of direction, or even just to have it confirmed that we are on the right track. I know I have benefitted from meeting people who have massively influenced my life, and my career; people whose knowledge ignited within me a passion and enthusiasm to make positive changes in my life.

They allowed me to discover just like my little wobbly friend, that I didn't have to keep sliding back down and that life was not always going to be up hill. Giving others a helping hand to make positive changes in their lives always gives me the same feeling I had when helping my little wobbly friend.

Photo taken by Emma Shawcross proud Mum of her daughter Bella.

Why did I write this book?

I've been presenting seminars and workshops on the psychology of leadership mastery for over twenty five years now. What I've found, working with some of the top UK and European companies, is that the same patterns keep emerging. This book is an introduction into some of those patterns, why they happen and more importantly how we can prevent them.

Have a look at how you could implement the differences when you read this book and take on board all its concepts, but more importantly transform its knowledge into positive action.

- What difference would it make to your career?
- What difference would it make to your home life?
- What difference would it make to your financial freedom?

You have the power within you to make the necessary changes that would enhance every area of your life.

Wouldn't it make perfect sense that, if you wanted to be happy, you would study happiness? If you wanted to be financially free, that you would study wealth? And if you wanted to a successful leader you would study people and their behaviours?

All of the things that I share with you in this book are transferable into all areas of your life, this is not just about your career. This will improve your home life. This will improve your finances. This will improve every aspect of any relationship that you have, both in work and out of work.

Like all skills, if you don't practice, and you don't make an attempt to put them into use on a daily basis, then unfortunately, they are not particularly helpful. So the onus now is on you, to make a commitment; a commitment that says to you, that you will at least try to use the skills and the information contained in the book.

If we look at it purely from a career point of view, to be the type of person that companies fight to keep, one of the main areas that we need to look at is the fact that most new managers believe they are paid for their time. People are not paid for time; people are paid to add value.

This is one of the most common mistakes that a lot of employees, managers, supervisors and leaders make. They think that they are getting paid for the time in which they are in work. But in actual fact, they are not. What they are paid for is to add value to the bottom line profit. If you are not adding value, then the harsh reality of life is the company does not need you. The skill of this book is to share with you insights in how you can become more valuable: the type of person that companies will fight to keep.

In the 1930's, Napoleon Hill wrote a book titled "Think and Grow Rich". The essence of the book was not solely focused on the word "rich" in the title; it's that it revolved around more than finances and money. In many ways, my book is exactly the same. Yes, it would be nice to have more money. It would be nice to have a very large bank account but because all of the skills that I share are transferable, then you really can think and grow rich in every area of your life.

Rich, but not just in a financial sense, in the sense that you could become the person that people could look up to, no matter how tall they grow or to be the best that you can be and to make that full connection to life. To be the best we can be we have to first take a look at ourselves.

Self-awareness is that most important skill that we need to examine. Out of forty-one thousand successful business leaders, who were tested for their emotional intelligence, self-awareness is the number one trait that they put down as important to their success.

The definition of self-awareness is: being conscious of what you're good at while acknowledging what you still have to learn.

Why is self-awareness so vital to our success?

Research by one of America's leading psychologists, Dr. Joyce Brothers, confirmed why this has to be the one all encompassing trait that determines your success. Dr. Brother's research can best be summed up in one great quote:

"You cannot consistently outperform the image you have of yourself".

What a powerful quote, when you begin to spend some time to contemplate and reflect on her words and her findings. Take a few minutes right now and reflect on her words; they are very powerful in influencing your success as a leader. *"You cannot consistently outperform the image you have of yourself".*

If we are self-aware of our internal self-image, we can make the changes. If we are self-aware of the feedback we are getting from people, positive or negative, we can adjust our course. That self-awareness is part of the journey we are going to go on. Because what I really want you to do as we go through this book, is to become far more self-aware. In order to change our self-image, to be able to outperform the image that we have, simply by altering and improving our self-image.

Many years ago, I had the privilege of working with young children, who had been expelled from main stream schools. My job was to help them change their image of themselves so that they could lead a more rewarding and successful life. I'd like to share with you a story that reflects Dr Joyce Brothers quote.

At the lunch times, all the boys in the school had to sit at tables where there were three or four boys and two members of staff. Each table took it in turn to go up to the food service counter to get their food. The boy, who was sitting next to me, twelve years of age, came back with his lunch in one hand, and a plate of bread in the other. He said to me, as he put the plate of bread down.

"Look at that sir; eighteen pence a loaf. It's not white; it's grey." He was 100% correct the bread looked several shades of grey but definitely not white. "Is this all we're worth Sir, eighteen pence a loaf?" Now bearing in mind with the prices, this was quite a considerable amount of money in its day. I never spoke to the young man. I just watched him and waited to see how this was going to develop and what he was going to do because as I said, these boys had already been expelled from main stream schools. Most of them had either emotional or behavioural difficulties. The boy did no more than turn around to the next table, and spoke to the Headmaster. He said, "Headmaster, Headmaster, do you think for Christmas we could have a Warburton's loaf?

The morale of this story is quite simple. If you look at the quote from Dr Joyce Brothers, she states that we cannot consistently outperform the image we have of ourselves. This young man, in his wisdom at twelve years of age, and with all of his problems and all of his insecurities in life, knew one thing; that the image set upon him of eighteen pence, wasn't going to get him through life, but the image of the price of a Warburton's loaf, which at the time was about ninety pence, would have helped him achieve more.

As a leader, manager, or supervisor, we constantly have to keep increasing our value. We have to keep improving our self-image, our sense of mastery that of being better today than we were yesterday.

As a manager what is your self-image like. Do you feel confident in you role?

- *If you were to give yourself a value like my young friend asking for a Warburton's loaf; what price would you value yourself at? Would you be 18 pence or would you be 90 pence?*

- *18 pence_____ 90 pence_____.*

- **Or would you be a loaf bought from Harrods at £5.00_____.**

This is exactly what we are trying to do by constantly being more self-aware, by using feedback to improve our self-image.

When we're working with people, we need to be aware of where their self-image is. Where is their thermostat set? Is it set at an eighteen pence loaf? In which case, you will only get eighteen pence worth of output from them. Or is it set at ninety pence? When we go back to being paid, not for time, but for adding value, if we could take every one of the people that we manage, and help them to grow better today than they were yesterday, help them develop from eighteen pence into ninety pence; then we are adding massive value. You really will become the person that companies fight to keep. Be the person people always will look up to you, no matter how tall they grow. You can be the best you can be, by helping others be the best they can be.

When I talk about being the person people can look up to, no matter how tall they grow. I'm going to ask you just to spend a few seconds thinking about all of the bosses, all of the leaders that you have had in your career so far.

Is there one that stands out from the rest? Is there one that stands out above all of the others? That one dynamic leader that you have the highest regard for and that you have the warmest feelings for?

What I'd like you to do is to make a list of their top five traits. What are the top five things that come to mind when you think about that leader, manager, that person you respect and look up to? What is it that they had, that you still value, respect and remember?

Top five traits:

1. _____.

2. _____.

3. _____.

4. _____.

5. _____.

From your list of 5 traits, how many relate to IQ and how many relate to emotional intelligence / people skills?

IQ:

—

—

—

—

EI:

—

—

—

—

I've used this technique of getting people to see that on average their previous bosses and managers, the ones that they respect, the ones that stand out for them, will have four out of the five competencies of their character traits relate to emotional intelligence, rather than IQ. If you look down your list, I'm sure you'll see things like: you felt trusted, he was honest or she was honest, you felt that they would be there for you; they could be firm and still fair. These are the most common things that people say about a successful manager or leader. The mere fact that you still remember them, and in some cases, that memory can go back twenty or thirty years, shows you that you can be the person that people look up to no matter how tall they grow. But also from a family sense, as we watch, develop and help our family grow, wouldn't it be nice that they looked up to you, no matter how tall they grew.

By developing that sense of self and developing our awareness, our self-awareness, of being conscious of what you're good at, while acknowledging what you still have yet to learn. By applying that same concept to the people that you manage and lead, you help yourself, and them, to be more emotionally connected in life.

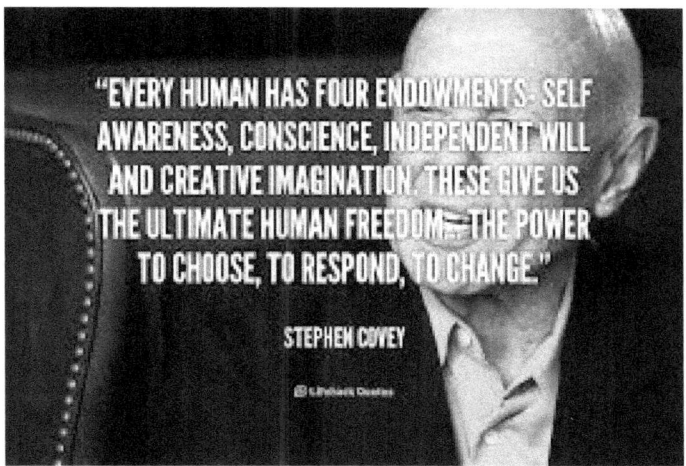

Life is never like a flat line, if it was, then there would be no movies and no books. As my mentor said, "Its hard to find a rich hermits". One of the most important areas that leaders and managers have to develop is employees is getting people to engage. The more people that engage, the harder they work. Not because you're trying to force them to do that, but because they want to do that.

Later in the book, we will look at different styles of motivation. The most important one is called intrinsic motivation; people want to do the task not because their being forced to.

So we've covered a lot of ground in this introduction, quite a long way about making a difference to your career.

Through the chapters of this book, some of the things that we're going to look at are how to generate a state of flow; that feeling you have when you're in that intrinsic motivated state where time passes and you want to just carry on and keep going.

What we are also going to look at is some of the profiles and success characteristics of one thousand two hundred and thirty-three of some of the most successful business owners. We are also going to look at 16,222 successful business people, managers just like you, whose character traits you can learn from, develop, and integrate into being better today than you were yesterday.

We are going to study different aspects of motivation so that we can develop that intrinsic motivation as well as look at the four stages of flow, that moment when you're "in that zone", the research comes from Professor Csikszentmihalyi his research included over 250,000 people across varying continents.

Everything that I share with you is tried, tested and proven, but more importantly, it's going to give you practical insight into how to become a better leader, manager and supervisor. Just like the pineapple, it's about developing the people around you, around that central core of the business, so that each and every one of them will be giving you the best they can give. When people give their best they naturally give their most.

Pineapple equals leadership

I am often asked why the pineapple represents leadership. I'd like to share with you the ten pineapple facts and how they relate to the psychology of leadership mastery.

We have already spoken about the fact that the pineapple is not one single fruit. But a hundred or more individual "fruitlets" that grow around the central core of the pineapple and then form one fruit. When I first discovered this fact, really allowed me to realise that the psychology of leadership mastery and the pineapple are very, very similar.

Our skill, ability and success as a leader, manager, or supervisor are based on how well we, all of our individual departments and the individual people in those departments come together around the central core of the business. There is another element too; that's how we develop ourselves. We have already discussed the fact that self-awareness is about being conscious of what you're good at while acknowledging what you still have to learn.

Leadership mastery is developing both the people around us, while we develop ourselves. That is the most important measure; because the more we develop ourselves, the greater heights we can take other people to.

In my first book, *"Great Leaders Never Climb Smooth Mountains"*, I talk about the seventeen and a half proven ways, seventeen and a half of the most annoying traits that members of staff have flagged up to me as being very annoying and frustrating. A half measure, is exactly what it is, it is about not giving half measures. It is about giving the best you can be.

It is about doing everything in your power to keep growing and developing. So, half measures do not cut it in today's modern world. Half measures are just not acceptable in today's market place.

The more that we can develop ourselves; the more we are then enabled to develop those people around us.

🍍 ***That is the first fact about the pineapple and how it relates to the psychology of leadership mastery.***

It is your ability to develop yourself and those you manage to work together around the central core of the business.

Exercise:

Where do you need to develop yourself in order to go from good to outstanding?

1. _____.
2. _____.
3. _____.

🍍 ***The second fact about a pineapple is:*** The pineapple originated in Spain and then the plants were eventually transferred to Hawaii. Hawaii is now the single biggest producer of pineapples in the world. Earlier in the book, I said to you that leadership is about transferring ideas from one mind to another. This is a great example of how great ideas can be transformed and then taken on to new areas.

For those of you who are not familiar with a gentleman called Ray Kroc, let me expalin, he was a milkshake machine salesman who noted that one of his customers was buying more machines than any of the others. Then one day, his customer rang him and said we need a machine that can dispense more than one milkshake at a time, because at our busy times we haven't got time to wait while one person is using the machine.

We need a milkshake machine that can dispense more than one flavour at the same time. Ray Kroc went out to meet these customers; Kroc was impressed with their fantastic business model. He said to the owners of the business, you really need to franchise this operation. The owners of the business said: "No, thank you. We are okay where we are. We are okay doing what we're doing."

Ray Kroc could see such massive potential in it that he bought out the owners. The owners were the McDonald brothers. Ray Kroc went on to become, the ninth most influential business person in America, as he owned the whole of the McDonald's Empire. So when you see those golden arches, and you stop in for a Big Mac, just remember; a transfer of ideas, like the pineapple travelling from Spain to Hawaii, allows us to grow even bigger and better.

Another such story is about Howard Schultz, who was a coffee bean salesman. He went to Milan to research and fact find about the business. What he noticed was that they were not just selling beans and coffee cups in Milan; they were selling actual cups of coffee. On most of the street corners, there was a coffee shop where people would come to sit and drink coffee brewed for them to their liking. He came back home and said to the company he was working for, "Here is a great idea. We should be branching out into selling cups of coffee, not just beans and cups."

But Howard Schultz ideas went basically unheeded. Nobody took those ideas forward and so he decided to set up Starbucks. When you look at the difference, just that simple transfer of ideas from one mind to another made, then you can see how the transfer of a pineapple from Spain to Hawaii created one of the biggest industries in Hawaii. When you look at the franchises of McDonald's, they are in every country in the world. The growth of the coffee industry and the coffee culture of people going out for a coffee, again a great idea transferred into someone else's mind. That is the difference in going from great to outstanding.

Exercise:

Look around your team who are the creative thinkers?

> Select 3 or 4 creative thinkers to form a mastermind group,

> Ensure that each member brings different strengths to the table.

I am regularly asked by companies to facilitate this type of group so that we can capture those great ideas and more importantly implement them.

Would your company / career benefit from?

> Doubling turnover,

> Increasing bottom line profit at no extra production costs?

> Opening up a new untapped market?

How valuable would you be as a manager / leader when you have achieved any one of the above?

🍍 *__Point three of the ten pineapple facts:__* The juice of the pineapple is used in medicine to induce child birth.

You might be wondering why childbirth relates to the psychology of leadership mastery. Sometimes we have got to go through a little pain, sometimes we need to experience things a little bit differently, in order for new growth to come. Like having a baby, it is worth it in the end. All of that pain, all of that suffering, is worth it, when that new little smiling face comes into the world.

If we can adopt all of the facts that you are going to read, develop and work with, as you work your way through this book. I'm hoping it induces people to work better, faster, easier; enabling you to have more success, more often and more easily, in particular, less stress, less hassle, and less frustration.

Exercise:

Which painful decisions have you been putting off?

1. _____.
2. _____.

What great ideas do you need to let germinate in the fertile soil of your mind?

1. _____.
2. _____.
3. _____.

Are you willing to share these ideas with your mastermind group?

> If the answer is No, why?

Point four of the ten pineapple facts: When you use the juice of a fresh pineapple, not a processed tin pineapple, but a fresh pineapple to make a jelly, you will find that the jelly will not set. The enzyme within the pineapple will not allow the jelly to set. In many ways, when we apply that to leadership mastery, we do not want our ideas to be fixed and set. We want to be constantly moving and fluid with our ideas.

We need to understand that what was successful last year, may not be successful this year. We need to constantly keep evolving from where we are now, to where we need to be.

As human being we are never stationary we are either moving forward or moving backwards.

In relation to the team you are leading today in which direction are the going?

Later in the book I am going to share with you the six laws of the mind; so that you can see how important this particular fact about the pineapple is regarding not having a fixed mind-set. It is massively important, because your mind is the greatest thing that you possess. It controls every aspect of your life from your financial freedom to your wealth. It controls every relationship that you have. Surely, you would want to know about the six laws of the mind, if it helps you to be the best you can be.

● *<u>Point five of the ten pineapple facts:</u>* Every part of the pineapple is used. When we apply this to the psychology of leadership mastery, it's about maximising our full potential. Not just ours but of all of those people around us. When we look at the aspects of creating that mind-set of flow that allows us to be totally absorbed in the project; at the end of the day, you can go home and think, what a great day that was, because you got from the day, not just through the day.

Maximising our potential, and those that we manage, lead or supervise, is absolutely vital and equally so for them, because the more they feel they are maximising their full potential, the more they will want to give. The more they will be willing to learn new techniques, new ideas, and more importantly, share those ideas with you.

🍍 *Point six of the ten pineapple facts:* It takes twenty-four months to fully develop a pineapple. When we look at leadership mastery, there is no "quick fix", there is no "one size fits all", or "one tablet" that you can take that would make its mastery instant. It is very much that process of better today than yesterday. Leadership mastery is a journey, not a destination; because we are constantly evolving, the way the world is constantly evolving, and technology is evolving. All of the business processes are getting faster and more efficient, we need to keep pace with them.

Rather than waiting a preset amount of time for it to develop, (as I've said, "mastery is a journey, rather than a destination") we can enjoy the benefit of that full potential every single day of our lives, not just once at the end of the 24 months.

🍍 *Point seven of the ten pineapple facts:* When sea captains used to return from their voyages, and would bring back pineapples, the first thing that they would do was to place some in a basket outside of their door. That was a symbol of two things: first the symbol of hospitality and second it was recognition that the sea captain was home and you were then welcome to visit. In architecture, if ever you see a pineapple on a building or, as is common in the Caribbean, on furniture, that is the symbol of hospitality.

When we apply that rule into leadership mastery, it's about having that open door policy.

- *Do people feel safe in coming to speak to you?*
- *Do people feel that they are made welcome with their ideas?*
- *Are you approachable or are you one of the closed door people?*

The one whose look just says, "Do not come in! Do not disturb!" Yes, there are times when we need to close our door and get stuck into a project or something that is quite pressing; but people need to feel safe and that it is okay to approach you.

You never know what great idea they might bring to the table. You never know how many great ideas have gone unsaid. They equally could have helped you in your career and your life, if we would have listened and been open. Are we approachable? If not, why not? What great ideas could you be missing by not being open?

🍍 *<u>Point eight of the ten pineapple facts:</u>* A pineapple can bear fruit for over 50 years. The Chartered Institute of Management estimates that it cost £65,000 to replace a senior manager. Not just in the fees, but in the breakdown of communication, and equally, the breakdown in customer relations. At one of the companies that I was recently working with, a senior executive could pinpoint a dip in their sales when a key executive had left the company. It maybe that £65,000 is a conservative estimate.

You want people to bear fruit for those fifty years. People will only bear fruit if they feel valued, respected, and that their ideas are listened to. When they feel that they have a connection with you, and the business that their working for.

Exercise:

Score yourself out of a possible 10 point; 10 being the top mark on the following questions:

- Your listening skills,

- If we asked each team member do they feel valued by you what score would they give you?

- Equally do they feel respected by you, what score would they give you?

What score would you give yourself for the same three points?

> Listening skills?_____.

> Making people feel valued?_____.

> Making people feel respected?_____.

🍍 ***Point nine of the ten pineapple facts:*** The pineapple juice contains magnesium. That gives us more energy. It also will improve your love life, but maybe that is for another book. Having that energy in the morning, where you spring out of bed and can do all of the things that you want to do. In eastern philosophy, they talk about the solar plexus energy. It is a little bit like a modern day Newton's cradle; one of those executive toys that you see on many desks, where there are steel balls suspended on fine wire. As you pick one of the steel balls up and let it go, it crashes into the other balls, and then creates a tremendous amount of movement. Solar plexus energy is self-generating, very similar to the Newton's cradle, but occasionally you just have to put a little more energy in and the energy that you put in is minimal to the energy that you get out.

If you do not have a Newton's cradle, I would suggest that you go out and get one because it will remind you that the more energy you have, the more momentum you can generate. Not only for yourself, but for those you manage, lead and supervise.

You will equally be aware of the fact that it is self-generating, and they will just keep gently adding more and more energy, all the time. When people are doing that for themselves, they will automatically give you their best. When people are giving their best, they will automatically give you their most.

🍍 ***Point ten of the pineapple facts:*** A pineapple is full of vitamin C. How does that relate to the psychology of leadership mastery? Quite simple, vitamin C helps to boost our immune system.

One of the things that happen when we are under stress is our immune system shrinks. If we can go through life with less stress, less hassle and less frustration; more success more often, more easily, then our immune system will be healthier. We will be healthier. Our work-life balance will be more in balance. If you're like the sea captain we mentioned in point seven and your door is open, then the truth is when people meet us we release endorphins. Endorphins make us feel better.

They help us to focus more, conversely, the opposite of that happens when we release a hormone called Cortisol.

Cortisol, when it is released into the body, affects our quality of thinking. It reduces all of our cognitive abilities. So if you're the type of manager, that rules by fear, all your doing is making people weaker, both physically and mentally, and affecting the bottom line profit. But the fact that you are reading this book, would indicate, that you're the type of leader that would encourage people to release endorphins.

As a leader, manager or supervisor, you need to light up the room by entering it, not when you leave it.

Exercise:

Re-read the quote above and ask yourself these two questions:

- Which of these do you do? _____.
- What is that you do to create this? _____.

The cost of stress and sickness is massively important, because lost through sickness is money that comes straight off our bottom line profit. These are the little things we can do, on a day to day basis, to help create a better work-life balance. Not just for ourselves, but for the people that work for us and with us.

You can begin to see how important the pineapple is, in terms of our leadership mastery.

As we go through the rest of this book, we are going to look at the five different hard-wire drives of the brain and how they relate to ourselves and the people we manage. I am going to show you the eight elements of how to add value, not time. Important aspects of how to get the best out of those people we manage and lead.

Above all, we can continue on our journey to be the person that companies fight to keep or to be the person people look up to, no matter how tall they may grow.

The fact that you're reading this book tells me that you want to be the best that you can be, and you want to make that emotional connection to life.

"You can design the most wonderful business in the world. But it takes people to make your dream a reality."

On a scale of 1-2-10: with 10 being fantastic, how well do you team work together? _____.

Who are individual people you work with who are showing you they are working as a team?

Who are the team members who are not working as a team?

People know what to do, so why the hell don't they do it?

I have been running workshops and courses for senior managers, on precisely this subject: People know what to do, so why the hell don't they just do it? The reason I do it this is, because this is the one of the questions that I am most frequently asked. Based on my work with hundreds of companies, I have noticed, that managers and leaders, consistently struggle with this question. In twenty-five years, of creating excellence within people, I can sum it up in one sentence.

"It's knowing how to be different that makes the difference."

I have proven time and time again, that individuals will improve their lives, and their careers, once they connect to the knowledge of how to be different, in order to actually be different.

How do we connect to the knowledge and how do we use it to our advantage. The good news is that we have in our possession the perfect goal achieving system in the world; you possess everything you need to be successful the sad thing is that we don't all know how to fully operate our goal achieving system.

Some people go through life constantly asking: **I know what to do so why the hell don't I do it?**

Our goal achieving system is a part of our brain called the Reticular Activating System (R.A.S.) let me explain;

What is the R.A.S.?

Imagine that you're walking through a busy noisy railway station. Think of all the noise - hundreds of people talking, announcements, the noise of the trains arriving and leaving.

How much of this noise is brought to your attention? Not a lot.

True, you can hear a general background noise, but not many of us bother to listen to each individual sound. Then a new announcement comes over the public address system - saying your name or maybe your train details.

Suddenly **your attention** is full on. Your reticular activating system is the automatic mechanism inside your brain that brings relevant information to your attention.

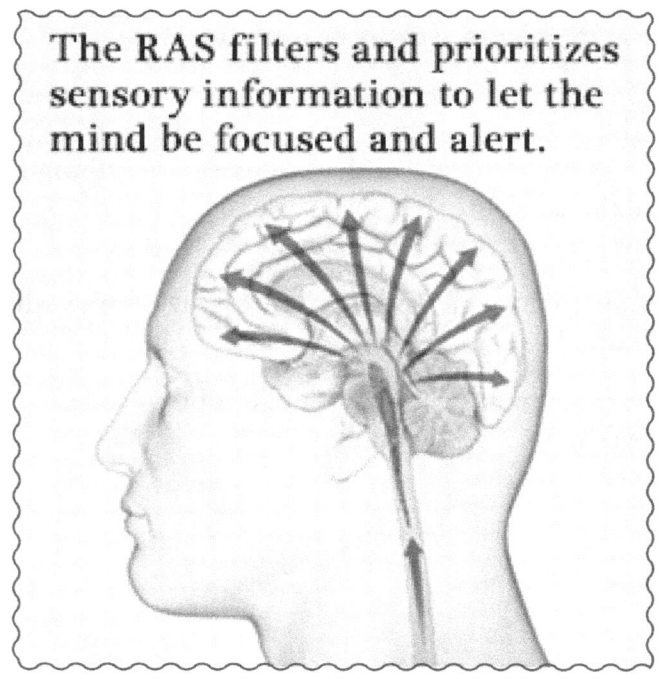

The RAS filters and prioritizes sensory information to let the mind be focused and alert.

Your R.A.S. is like a filter between your conscious mind and your subconscious mind. It takes instructions from your conscious mind and passes them on to your subconscious. For example, the instruction might be, "Listen out for anyone saying my name".

There are some interesting points about your R.A.S. that make it an essential tool for achieving goals.

First, you can intentionally **program** the R.A.S. by choosing the exact messages you send from your conscious mind. For example, you can **set goals**, or **visualise** your goals.

Second, your R.A.S. cannot distinguish between 'real events' and 'synthetic' reality. In other words it tends to believe whatever message you give it. Imagine that you're going to be giving a speech. You can practice giving that speech by visualizing it in your mind. This 'mental' rehearsal will improve your ability to give the speech.

What we need to do is to create a very specific picture of our goal in our conscious mind. The R.A.S. will then pass this on to our subconscious - which will then help us achieve the goal. It does this by bringing to our attention all the relevant information which otherwise might have remained as 'background noise'.

You've heard it time and time again – write down your goals as it will increase the chances of you achieving those goals. There is research that shows that when you write your goals down and post them in visible places to remind yourself of those goals, you will be more able to achieve those goals.

The reality is that we only have a limited amount of energy and attention to direct toward our goals. Evolutionarily speaking, our brain is designed to conserve energy. We're either focusing on:

1. Dealing with threats in our environment and learning how to put out fires, or

2. Focusing on ways to master our environment and work toward higher order goals that are important to our well-being.

Exercise:

> What % of your day is spent in dealing with threats and putting out fires?

> What % of your day is focusing on mastery?

Obviously with goal achievement, we are more interested in the latter, learning how to master our environment by achieving our goals, because it brings us pleasure, rewards, life satisfaction and of course some degree of security as well.

A key factor that prevents us from staying focused on our goals, and achieving those goals is that it's hard to direct our attention on those goals *all the time* or often enough. There are so many distractions and demands in our everyday life, that it seems almost impossible to stay focused at times. Our R.A.S. helps make the process of paying attention and being focused a little bit easier.

Specifically, research in goal setting and motivation states that our arousal systems help us focus on our goals. The reason we have arousal systems to begin with is that evolution has hard wired us to conserve energy, and we are only meant to be aroused when we have a concrete reason – protecting our safety in some fashion or increasing our resources in some way.

Our brain only gets super focused if and when it needs to, otherwise, just like a computer, one could argue that it goes to sleep and does the minimal amount of work needed. When a person has no clear goals, doesn't write their goals down and doesn't have plans to achieve those goals, their level of goal arousal, passion and overall enthusiasm is low. As a result, they do not recognise or identify the people, opportunities, situations or resources that could be helpful to them.

How do we increase our levels of arousal to help us achieve our goals? By learning how to activate your R.A.S. which is part of your cortical arousal system, you can increase your chances of being much more efficient with your goals.

So what role does writing our goals down play in helping us to achieve our goals? By writing down your goals and your plans for achieving your goals, you learn to focus your attention on what really matters. Doing so gets your reticular activation system aroused and working in your favour.

How does this work? When you write down your goals, you make a point of being specific with a direction that is important for you to move in. You pinpoint specific destinations that you want to move toward, and the specific steps that you need to take to get there.

As you get in touch with what is exciting and rewarding to you, you increase your levels of arousal, and become crystal clear about what matters. As you are doing this, your R.A.S. in your cortex is aroused and promotes you being ready and alert to respond to cues in the environment that are relevant to your goals. When the R.A.S. is activated, we can process and reorganise information much more efficiently in ways that support our achievement of goals.

A classic yet simplified example of your R.A.S. working would be when you identify an article of clothing that you would like to purchase. You try on a beautiful blouse and you write down the size, brand, colour and store where you found it. In the meantime, as you are waiting for it to go on sale, you see other people wearing that blouse because now you are primed to spot it!

You'll also recognize similar types of blouses perhaps by other designers. Your brain is automatically aroused when it notices this blouse because you have indicated that it is something important to you. The same thing happens when you identify a new car that you want to buy.

You begin to notice that car everywhere, because you've signaled the importance of this car to your brain.

The R.A.S. is the attention center in the brain. It is the key to "turning on your brain," and also seems to be the center of motivation.

In other words, it is the part of your brain where the world outside of you, and your thoughts and feelings from "inside" of you, meet.

The R.A.S. and Learning

The R.A.S. plays a significant role in determining whether a person can learn and remember things well or not, or whether or not a person is impulsive or self-controlled, and on whether or not a person is highly motivated or bored easily.

When functioning normally, it provides the neural connections that are needed for the processing and learning of information, and the ability to pay attention to the correct task.

If the R.A.S. doesn't excite the neurons of the cortex as much as it ought to, then we see the results of an under-aroused cortex, such as difficulty learning, poor memory, little self-control, and more worryingly we are caught up the never ending cycle of people go through life constantly asking:

I know what to do so why the hell don't I do it?

Which in turn leads to managers and leaders constantly asking?

"People know what to do, so why the hell don't they do it?"

Helping those we manage and lead to fully understand our R.A.S. will help us add value to the bottom line while allowing us to be more successful more often more easily with less stress less hassle and less frustration.

Why is it so vital for us to help ourselves and those we manage to eliminate compare these research findings?

➤ 89% of employees have switched off within six months of joining a company.

🍍 What % of your team has switched off _____%

➤ 87% of employees said that they could do significantly more, in relation to their job.

› More frighteningly, 74% said, that they wanted to do more.

🍍 What are the names of your team do you feel would want to do more?

Where does this contradiction come about? That 87% of employees said that they could do more and 74% said they wanted to do more, and yet 89% of employees have switched off within 6 months of joining a company.

It comes from the fact that as a leader we either manage people well or we fail. Our job as leaders, managers, and supervisors, is to help people know how to be different and to be like pineapple, to come together around the core of the business.

Deep down, there are 5 hard-core drives, in the human brain. As a leader, we need to understand these hard-core drives, and how they relate to change management and the success of programming the reticular activating system.

If we do not understand how to be different we won't be adding value at the first attempt. Instead, we will have to redo, resend, or refund. In order to help you to understand the benefit of change management, and in particular, we will look in depth at the five hard-wire drives of the human brain, and how they relate to the psychology of leadership mastery, and in particular, your success.

Everything You Need To Learn About Leadership You Can Learn From A P1NEAPPLE

To introduce the five hard wired drives, I am going to use the acronym B-L-A-D-E, but first let me give you an insight into the fascinating world of the human body and how it is hard wired for success and achievement.

The human heart starts beating in an unborn foetus before the brain has been formed. Scientists refer to this phenomenal fact as auto-rhythmic, meaning the heart is self-initiated from within the heart. Neuroscientists also refer to this as the brain in the heart or the heart's intrinsic brain.

The most important word in this section is the word "intrinsic" in relation to motivation a topic we will cover later in the book.

Intrinsic motivation is defined as: doing an activity for the sheer pleasure and satisfaction of doing it, rather than, some external reward or punishment. When intrinsically motivated, a person is moved to act, for the sheer fun and pleasure that simple challenge entailed, rather than because of an external pressure, or reward, or punishment.

I was ecstatic to discover that my heart has an intrinsic brain and that it takes sheer pleasure and satisfaction in beating 100,000 times per day while pumping two gallons of blood per minute, the equivalent of over 100 gallons per hour through the 60,000 miles of my vascular system. **WOW!**

How can we benefit from understanding that we have not only an intrinsic heart but we also have five hard wired drives that can either re-enforce or eliminate the frustration of:

"People know what to do, so why the hell don't they do it?"

To introduce the five hard wired drives, I am going to use the acronym B-L-A-D-E.

● **The B stands for belong.** Belonging is the first of the five hard-wire drives that neuroscientists have identified. These five hard-wire drives have universally transcended all ages, status, and cultures. They are as I said, hard-wired. So the benefit of a leader to understand these, will allow us to understand the people that we work with, as well as understanding ourselves better.

Everything You Need To Learn About Leadership You Can Learn From A P1NEAPPLE

Our drive to belong originates from the time of our birth when you think of a new born baby, new born babies, and are totally co-dependent. Babies cannot look after themselves, they cannot get food, change their clothes, turn the heating up, they cannot go to the cooker and cook something. Our very basic instinct, early on in life, is to become connected to other human beings. That has to be hard-wired, without it we just would not survive.

When you look at today's modern social media, how people now are on Twitter, Facebook, WhatsApp, all of those things that they have to connect with each other, on multi levels. When you look around, if we have a natural progression, if you're interested in a particular sport, or you have a certain hobby, that you want to become a member of a club, or join together with like-minded people. I live in the Yorkshire Dales; I live out in the country where streetlights are a luxury One of the aspects about living in the Dales, in the early evening, just as its going dusk, you can constantly see the bats flying, using the lights from the house to pick out the insects they want for dinner.

I recently picked up a magazine that was the hundredth edition of the "Bat News". As you can see by this example even the most strange of hobbies, or the most general of hobbies, people still want to belong and come together.

Not every person works, just for money. Some people work for the social interaction, for the connection of being able to get out of the house, and to meet with other people. So as a leader, manager, or supervisor, it is vital, that we understand the very nature, of why we need to belong.

When I said at the beginning of this chapter, the example of a new born baby, how it is born totally co-dependent, but in its journey through life, one of the major important factors that a baby has to learn, is to go from co-dependency to independency. We only learn that by going through the process of learning new ideas, and yet still connecting with other people, because in many cases, it is those other people that will be sharing those ideas with us.

🔹 **This leads us on to the L in the acronym of BLADE.** That is, we have a hard-wired desire to continue learning. That helps us complete the journey from co-dependency, to independency. It allows us to continue to be better today, than we were yesterday. It is that drive that pushes us, to learn new skills. It motivates us it gets us out of bed in the morning.

Everything You Need To Learn About Leadership You Can Learn From A P1NEAPPLE

Once again the fact that you're reading this book, tells me that you have already in you, that hard-wire drive to learn more.

It is said there are only three reasons why people do not change. Three beliefs that they may have; **the first one** is that they do not know how to change. **The second** belief, which is they do not have the self-confidence, or the self-esteem to learn new skills.

As you may have probably seen in your career, there are certain people who you know, could achieve far more. Yet, they have talked themselves out of it. They are in a way, their own worst enemy. Everybody else can see their potential, other than themselves.

The third reason is that sometimes people just do not want to change. Dr Bandler's expressed this in his quote "some people would rather die than change". Smoking is a great example of some people not wanting to change, they are willing to die rather than change, we need to help people to see the benefits of change support them in learning new skills.

Exercise:

> list your team members in the first column.

> In the other three columns tick what you believe is that team members beliefs about their level of skill?

Name	Belief one	Belief two	Belief three

● **The A stands for acquire.** We are constantly looking to acquire material, and nonmaterial things. If you think back, in your own life, how many houses you may have lived in, or rented. Every time, we are always trying to improve, and get bigger and better. It is the same with cars. It is the same with most possessions.

Everything You Need To Learn About Leadership You Can Learn From A P1NEAPPLE

For some people material possessions, it is vastly important to them. For some people it is a status symbol that they live in a bigger house, drive a bigger car. Have a car with the better interior, which has leather seats, air conditioning, or cruise control. Certain people take great pride in their post code, why it's because a post code gives them that feeling of status. Some times when you ask people, where they live, they are quite happy to give you their post code first, and then give you an approximate idea, of where in the country that is.

For some people, it is non-material. It purely is about status. I once knew a gentleman who went to see his boss for a pay rise, and was adamant that he was not coming out without a pay raise. But when he came out, he came out with a title that made him sales manager, had new responsibilities, and had extra work to do. But he didn't come out with a pay raise. He just came out with a badge that said sales manager. For him that was massively important, for his status and his influence.

Influencing how you transfer ideas from one mind to another, will determine your success a leader. So understanding how we influence, and how people acquire that influence, is quite important. In the one day seminars that I run, I go into this in more detail.

For some people they need, to acquire power. Power is neither good nor bad. It is what you do with the power that is important. A great example would be too examine the power that somebody like Mother Teresa had, or Dr Martin Luther King, now let's look at the misuse of power from somebody like, an Adolph Hitler. All three had the opportunity to use power for the greater good; unfortunately the latter misused the power with devastating consequences.

As a leader and as a manager, we have to understand, first of all, what is it that people are looking to acquire within their own lives. Seek first to understand and then to be understood, then we can begin to help other people, by developing them to acquire the skills, in order to help bring about positive change.

🔸 **The D in our acronym, stands for defend;** defend does not always have to have a negative connotation. When I go into a company, when I set up a mentoring program, I try to go that extra mile; I try to give 100%, every single time, why because I want to defend both my reputation, and equally acquire more status within the industry. So for me, defence can also be very positive. Because I want to achieve, I want to be the best I can be therefore it is very important, for us to defend our sense of self.

Everything You Need To Learn About Leadership You Can Learn From A P1NEAPPLE

I was once asked to teach a program for stress and anxiety management for business owners. I was currently running that program that took a week to cover the full content, in total five working days. A company asked me if I would do that in ONE DAY, and they wanted it done from 10:00 in the morning, till 4:00 in the afternoon; with a break in the morning, a break for lunch and a break in the afternoon. I quite happily said to them, that I could not possibly do that, and do the content or the participants justice. I had to defend my reputation and the quality and standard of the work people have come to expect from me.

Some people see defence purely in the negative sense; you see people who sometimes are stuck, almost in a constant mode of survival. They have a poor mind-set when they are asked to make any changes. They want to protect, and stay, in their little comfort zones. They will defend that comfort zone.

Modern science has told us, that the cells in our body have three main functions. The first one is to survive, and that's great. The second one is for each cell, to be able to reproduce. Certain cells only live for a few days, and other cells live up to 7 years in our body. As those cells reproduce themselves, for example you will have had 184 pairs of new eyes, in the last 12 months. Our cells need to survive, and they need to reproduce. The third and most important function is we are designed to reach our true potential. We are not meant to be stuck in survival mode. Defence can be very positive, but it can also be very negative and limiting Not only in our own careers, but in the careers of those that we manage.

Andrew Carnegie, the American steel magnate, was once asked when he was making his fortune, why is it you have more millionaires working for you, than any other company? Andrew Carnegie said: "Yes, and isn't it interesting, that none of them were millionaires when they came to work for me." You see, he did not have a survival mentality; he did not try to defend the fact that he didn't know certain things. What he actually decided was that he would staff his weakness. Anything he didn't know or understand, he would bring people in. Very similar to the pineapple, the whole aim was to bring everybody around the central core of the business, so everybody could grow and everybody could reach their true potential.

❂ **The E in BLADE** is that most people want to connect with other humans, just as we said right at the beginning of this chapter. It is about having an emotional experience. We do not want to go through life, with no ups and no downs. Life is not a flat line.

If you're a Star Trek fan, can you imagine what life would be like if we were all like Mr. Spock; very logical, but no emotive content whatsoever. A more modern day version of Mr Spock can be found on the American sitcom, the Big Bang Theory. If everybody was like Sheldon Cooper, then life would be pretty dull and boring. Even with his two doctorates, he still cannot connect to other human beings.

We have talked about flow. That state of feeling as though, when you're in the moment and time just passes and you're doing the work with that intrinsic motivation. That is about fully connecting emotively.

One of the best, most wonderful stories about people connecting together concerns a major incident that happened a few years ago, you may remember, the Chilean miners.

Thirty-three miners were trapped half a mile underground, when the rescuers came, they could not get into the mine because of the danger of further roof falls. The rescuers were worried if they removed the blockage that the roof might collapse on these thirty-three miners.

What the mine owners did, and the Chilean president did, was to bring in help; to bring in support teams. I am going to ask you a question, you may or may not remember this, but while the Chilean miners were still trapped, where was the Chilean president, when the rescue was taking place? The answer is; he was at the mine head.

He was there trying to help reassure the families and the people, that everything was being done. The Chilean government brought in all of the necessary help, all of the experts, the expert drillers they brought in a nutritionals, so that they could send the right food down to the miners. When they put a very small tube in that they could send water and parcels of food. They brought in a submarine commander to give them advice, on what it is like living, in a confined space. They used psychology, insight and wisdom of a submarine commander to help protect the miners state of mind.

As they were drilling the shafts to release the men, they realised that the size of the cage that would bring the miners to the surface, shaped like a little cigar tube created a problem.

What they discovered was, with the size of the hole they were drilling, they realised they needed a dietician, to get advice and the right foods, because the maximum waist size was 35 inches. If your waist was bigger than 35 inches, you would not have fit in the cigar tube that would have brought you back to the surface.

Again this story reminds me of the pineapple where everybody is pulling together, everybody wanting to be there, and going that extra mile not just for the thirty-three guys who were underground, but for the emotional connection.

I remember sitting up all night, watching the news reports, as the first of the miners were brought up to the surface. But there was one great emotional connection that I will never forget not just the joy and relief of see those miners being brought to the surface.

The moment I will always remember is the paramedic, who first left the safety of the ground, to go down for the very first time, half a mile. This was ensuring that he could help, and support the miners that were still trapped. The paramedic wanted to be sure that they were healthy enough, and fit enough, that they could get into the little cigar tube, to be brought back to the surface. I am not really too sure if I would have had the bravery, or the commitment, to leave the safety of the surface, and get into that tube to go down.

Having said that I think if I was a paramedic, and my job was to help save human life, and maybe that emotional connection, would have overridden any other fear or doubt that I may have had.

When we make a connection with people, we are always willing to go that extra mile. If your best friend rang you and asked you for a favour, you would do it. If somebody you did not know asked you, you probably would not be likely to do it. If somebody has been there to support you, you are more likely to help them when they need help.

Everything You Need To Learn About Leadership You Can Learn From A P1NEAPPLE

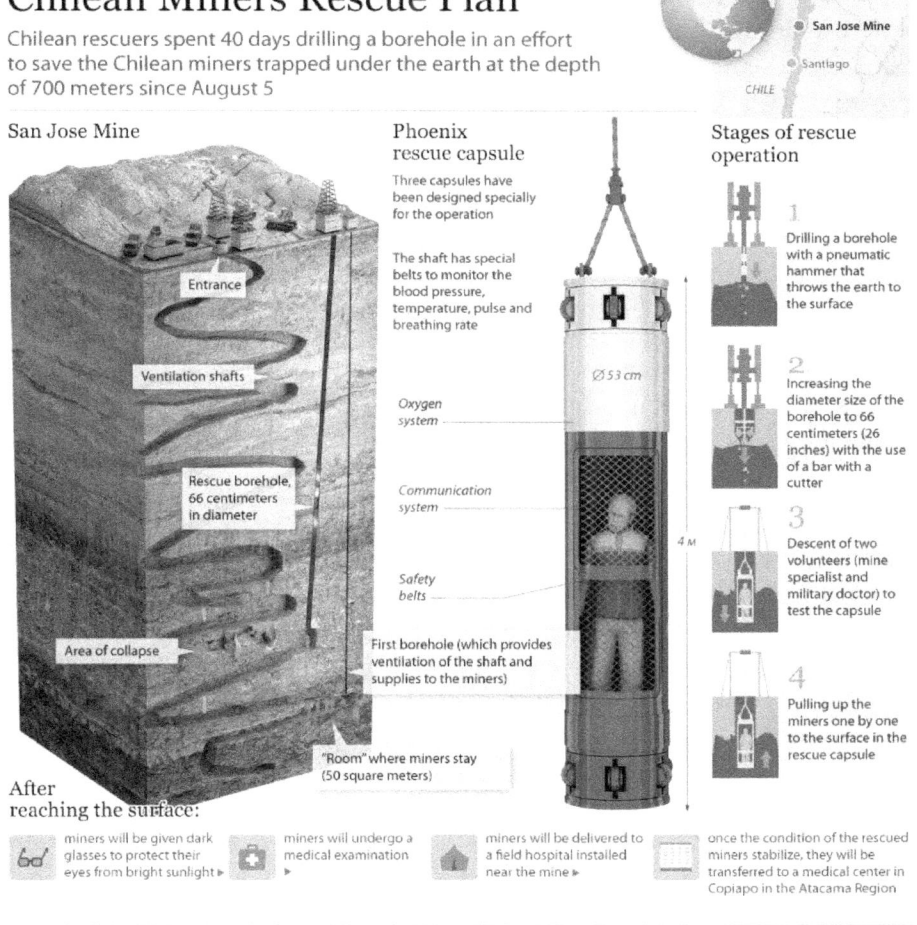

I asked you a question a few sentences ago that said, where was the Chilean president when all of that was going on? He was at the mine head, dressed in his jeans, and his leather bomber jacket so he could connect to the people.

A few weeks after that, there was horrendous floods in Pakistan, where a half million people were homeless. A few days after these floods had started, and people were already homeless, where was the Pakistani president? He had left the country while all of this was going on, and flew to London. To have his photographs taken, outside a big five star hotel, in London, with his immaculately cut suit.

You see, when people make an emotional connection, between the Chilean president and the Pakistani president, if that was your boss, and they were your leader, who would you go the extra mile for?

When human beings make a connection, there is a little part of the brain call the amygdala it record all of the emotions around us. The amygdala is capable of firing off at two hundred and fifty miles an hour, and is designed to save our life. The amygdala recalls all of the emotions around a certain event. If the amygdala is happy, it will process it then pass the information on to the thalamus. The thalamus is like a little filing cabinet in the brain. That has all of the facts to do with the incident that, the amygdala has passed on. If the amygdala is happy, we can then spend time looking for all of the facts. But if the amygdala is frightened, scared, or nervous, we do not have time to look at all the facts. We start making snap decisions we react rather than respond.

Developing an emotional connection with people, allows them to appease every aspect of their being because they get a sense of belonging. They will get a sense of, it is okay to learn, and it's okay to ask questions. We can develop their motivation within them. And in doing so, they can acquire that status that they need. It has once been said, that as a leader, you are either building self-esteem, or you are destroying it. As long as people are acquiring self-esteem they will always perform better. They will always perform at their best. If they are doing their best, they will always give you their most.

People will look to defend that relationship. People will look to stand up and say, I want to be with the Chilean president. I want to walk with him, because that guy probably will have my back. I am not saying that the Chilean president is the best president in the world, and the Pakistani president is the worst. I am just showing the difference, how when we connect to somebody or a cause, we want to go that extra mile.

It is vitally important that we get these drives right because if any one of these drives is missing, what that sets up in the brain is called, zeigarnik effect. The zeigarnik effect is, if we are not allowed to complete a task, a project, it develops within us a sense of frustration. If we are repeatedly not allowed, or hindered, we are not given the tools or the information to complete a job, what does that do to our motivation? It simply just switches it off, slowly, piece by piece.

A really great quote, that I have used an awful lot in my life, to help me and help those around me is, "resistance is a lack of clarity" when people are resisting change, it's really worthwhile to know, that that's predominantly a lack of clarity in them. If you go back to these five elements, these five hard-wired drives, there will be one, if not more of them missing. If you can understand that, and begin to break that down, speak to them, and find out which one of the five drives that is missing, then we can break down the resistance. When we gain clarity, we will be willing then to continue and make changes. As I said earlier in this chapter, getting it right first time is always better than redo, resend or refund.

Exercise:

> List your staff names,

> Reflect on their individual character,

> Which of the five hard wired drives do you feel need to be developed.

> Develop a plan that will help each person be better today that they were yesterday.

Name	Belong	Learn	Acquire	Defend	Emotional connection

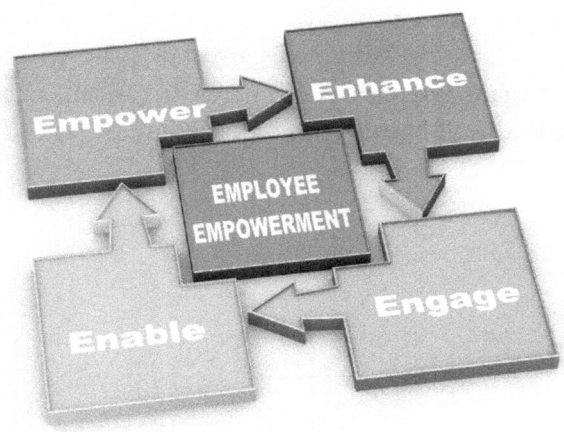

How to Add Value

What is leadership, and more importantly, what is leadership mastery, and how does it help us to add value? Leadership mastery is a step by step system to involve, inspire and ignite bottom line profits by creating excellence in people.

In this new era, either leadership executives manage people well, or they fail. Good leaders are the enabling force helping individuals and organisations to increase bottom line profit through the alignment of people's needs and the aims of the organisation. The leadership mastery system will enable those who manage others to achieve remarkable results; through developing the ability to cultivate the attitudes and behaviours which characterize, and relate to creating excellence in people.

Leadership mastery highlights how leadership is different to management. Management is being concerned with processes, while leadership is mostly about behaviours. Good leadership requires deeper human understanding, not necessarily great technical or intellectual capacity. These attributes might help, but they are not essential. Leadership mastery is solely concerned with creating excellence in people, while acknowledging that leadership involves decision making and taking action relating to technical processes within the business. All great leaders require one thing, followers. A successful leader's role is the ability to respond to people's needs and the constant challenges that this modern, complex and fast changing business world requires.

A-D-D-V-A-L-U-E.

In order to add value we first need to understand how invaluable our part in developing people is in a constantly changing, fast moving business world.

You either manage people well or you fail as a leader is a powerful mantra to have. Remember, there are no rich hermits and likewise leaders need people to lead who want to go in the same direction as the leader is going in.

If we examine this concept and we look back at our formal education, from the age of four or five we attend school full-time and we stay in school until the age of 16. All this time we are gaining our general education, what used to be called the 3 R's: reading writing and arithmetic.

We then go onto college and possibly university where our education becomes more precise and is formed around particular subjects. When we leave University and start employment, our employer will continue to develop our skills even further. In my profession and as a member of the The British Psychology Society, continuous professional development is an essential part of my development.

We spend 20 plus years gaining our general and specific education but nowhere are there formal training courses that teach people the skills or know how to get the best from those they spend time with whether at work or at home. Nowhere are there specific training programmes that teach leaders and managers how our brain is hard wired or how to understand people so that we involve, inspire and ignite them.

Earlier we talked about the 5 hard wired drives, now let's move on to the 8 major components that help us to add value to the lives of the people we manage, to add value to our career and to add value to the bottom line profit that ensures we become leaders that companies fight to keep.

The following 8 points should be blended with our knowledge of the 5 hard wired drives in order to help create excellence within people.

Introducing the acronym: A.D.D.V.A.L.U.E.

🍍 **The A stands for action,** not just any action but more importantly, transforming knowledge into positive action. All of the knowledge and the research contained within this book, and that we have gained throughout life is meaningless unless we can transform that knowledge in to positive action.

The action that we need to take is to understand the hard-wire drives and how we can share them in order to encourage people to embrace them and take them on as their own. So the A stands for action; to transform knowledge into positive action.

I recently worked with a golf professional and during one of our sessions I asked him what it was that transformed an average player into a more confident and professional golfer.

His answer was both profound and very simplistic: "If you have ever been to a golf driving range and watched people hitting golf balls, you'll notice that the majority pay their money for a bucket of 50 or 100 balls.

They then proceed to hit the balls without any supervision, instruction or guidance. What they are actually doing is practising their faults 50 or 100 times, they have becoming experts at not being successful. Whereas when we have supervision, instruction or guidance we are partaking in positive action not negative action."

I valued this insight personally as it related to all areas of my life because I became very conscious that without the right help and guidance the very last thing that I wanted to do was to be practising faults.

As a manager, leader or supervisor, understanding and implementing the five hardwire drives in addition to the information contained in A.D.D.V.A.L.U.E., you will be practising how to create excellence within people and more importantly, you will manage people well and avoid the consequences of failure.

Summary: "Our actions must be positive"

There's a wonderful Japanese proverb that says "Vision without action is a daydream and action without vision is a nightmare."

We can all be busy fools, but real growth only comes when all of our actions have a vision, a purpose and a positive content for ourselves, the people we manage and the company we all work for.

When I work with the leadership team of any company I see myself as one of the team and their goals becomes mine. I want to fully understand both the company and the people within it. I find the positive action needed to involve, inspire and ignite all three elements: the individual, the company and myself around their goals and aims.

❱ The D stands for direction. As a leader, manager, or supervisor, we should constantly be learning lessons from previous great leaders and managers. One in particular, my personal hero in life, is Dr. Martin Luther King. His direction was guided by three main components.

1. Is it constructive?

2. Is it positive?

3. Does my action take us in the direction we want to go?

There are two key words in the third component; the words US and WE they are focused on collaboration not just self interest. compare the collaborative version of the third component: Does my action take US in the direction WE want to go in?

Now compare the self interest version:

Does my action take ME in the direction I want to go in?

Using the formula that Dr. King used with great success then every action that we undertake should be founded on his three principles;

Is it constructive?

I'm sure like me you have spent time in a relationship that was not constructive. It may well have been constructive for them but it was anything but mutually constructive. The only way we build mutually constructive relationships is to apply Dr Kings three principles.

Is it positive?

Not all relationships can be classed as positive. There are people whose actions have a negative impact on those around them.

Does my action take us in the direction that we want to go?

In quantum physics, the theory is that we are never standing still, we are either moving forwards or backwards. It is therefore vital that all of our actions have a forward positive motion, anything less than that and we are without doubt moving backwards and so is our career, our life and our relationships.

Summary: If you evaluate all your relationships and the answer to any of the following 3 questions is "No"; then stop, re-evaluate and more importantly, take the necessary action that gets you moving in the direction you want and need to go in.

- Is your entire communication 100 % Positive? Yes or NO?
- Is all of your communication 100% constructive? YES or NO?
- Is your leadership style focused on WE rather than I? YES or NO?

🍍**The second D is for dedicated practice.** As I have already explained, the natural default position of the mind is chaos and that it loves to have a process, a structure and a plan.

Here is an exercise to highlight the difference with and without a structure and a process:

All you will need is a pen and you watch or phone to time 60 seconds.

Look at the chart below in 60 seconds circle as many numbers in chronological order as possible in the 60 second; starting with the number one up to ninety.

	37		13		44	16		96	60	
61		57		29		48	52	84	32	
	97		65		24					
	69	1 9	25	45	21	8	20	100	40	56
85	73	49	93	89 41	5	68	4 12	72	28	92 80	88
	17	33	81	77	53	36		64	76	
	22	46 10	74	70	34		39	51	35	19	3
	82		18	58	54	7 43	11	31	63	55
	50	38	2	26	98	67	59	91	27	71
66	14	30	94	62	86	95	23 87	75	79	99
	42	6		78		15		83	47	

How well did you do, how many numbers did you circle?

_____

Now look at the chart again, you will notice two things:

› The chart is now divided into four.

› There is an arrow showing you a direction to follow: anti-clockwise.

- *Number one is in the top left quarter,*
- *Number two is in the bottom left quarter,*
- *Number three is in bottom right quarter,*
- *And number four is in the top right quarter.*

Now you know the structure and process redo the exercise, giving yourself 60 seconds.

Compare your original score with the structure and process compared to having the structure and process.

› Original score with no structure and process, _____.

› Second Score with structure and process, _____.

✓ As you can clearly see your were more successful more easily.

We have talked about one of my private clients, the golf professional. I asked him what the difference was between the average golfer and somebody like himself, who earns his living from playing golf. He said that the answer was in dedicated practice.

On a driving range, people invest their money in a bucket full of balls, and then they stand there hitting them one after the other with no help, no supervision, nobody to correct them. He went on to explain that when he was at Golf Pro school, they would hit 1000 golf balls a day, each shot had a purpose, a structure and was supervised. What was the point in practicing faults?

I thought his explanation of dedicated practice was absolutely mind blowing. That is exactly what most managers who do not understand the principles of leadership mastery are doing; practicing their faults which in turn will alienate and switch off those they manage.

Summary: Within the psychology of the leadership mastery mentoring program, what we are doing is creating dedicated practice. Practice that has a specific process, a structure, and plan, that is based on tried and tested methodology, which is proven by 12333 of the most successful business people, and 16222 of the world's most successful business managers and leaders.

You see understanding dedicated practice and transforming knowledge into positive action aimed at being constructive, positive, and going in the direction that we need to go in, is remarkably straight forward when you can follow the plans laid down by previous successful people. More importantly, there is one more thing we need to do, we need to be able to understand how our actions influence the actions of others.

🔸 **The V in my acronym stands for voice.** The people that we lead and manage need to feel that they have a voice. They need to feel that they are valued. None of these insights cost us any money. They just take a little bit of time, early on, for us to implement. But the time invested in learning and using them will return to you tenfold. You will have more time because you will have less hassle, less stress, and less frustration; leading to more success, more often and more easily.

People need to have a voice. They don't always have to have that voice turned into action, they just need to be able to feel valued and free to say exactly what's on their mind. It helps us to build rapport and deepen the quality of the relationship.

As we said earlier about the Chilean miners, if we can build a better rapport, a better relationship, people will go that extra mile for us. Whereas, if we don't have rapport, people will not want to share ideas, they will not want to come and say to us that they have a great idea or ask for our opinion on things.

I am fascinated to discover how many great ideas have gone unsaid. How many great careers have been lost as a result of people not feeling safe or valued enough to share such thoughts with their managers and supervisors.

Everything You Need To Learn About Leadership You Can Learn From A P1NEAPPLE

Earlier in the book, we talked about Ray Kroc and Howard Shultz, and the great ideas that were shared but not always picked up by others. Ray Kroc picked it up, and so did Howard Shultz's and they transformed it into a fortune. Like somebody transferring the idea of taking a pineapple from Spain to Hawaii and then having a multi-billion pound industry grow out of it as a result. When people have a voice, they feel as if they can belong. They feel as though they can learn more and acquire more. They feel that they can defend their point of view in a positive and helpful way. Then they can connect with people.

I run several groups for business owners, on the mastermind principle, where we meet once a month. I facilitate each group, helping them all to grow, both individually and in their business. Quite like the strands of a rope, when they are braided together, the strength is far greater than that of the individual strands. Ten minds are far more powerful than one mind. The whole is greater than the sum of the parts.

I am also a member of a mastermind group where our five minds braid together to help create excellence within each individual member.

Summary: You need to encourage people to express their voice and their opinions, so they feel valued and will share their ideas, because we cannot see everything and know everything.

Sometimes, people who see things differently can come up with the simplest ideas that turn out to be the most productive; like my golf professionals' dedicated practice routine.

◗ **The A stands for being authentic.** In a survey, only 46% of employees said that their manager's actions were congruent with their words. This is a very poor reflection on the managers who think they are fooling people regarding being authentic. The Chilean president is a great example of a leader being authentic. To be at the problem head, not to be on a plane, or in a country thousands of miles away, while the people that you serve are suffering.

Earlier in the book, I asked you to list the top 5 traits of the managers or leaders that you praised highly and remember the most. When you read back on that list, as I am going to encourage you to do right now, you may not have written the word authentic, but I am sure you will agree, that being authentic made them top of your list. When people are authentic, those that they manage and lead will always want to go that extra mile as opposed to becoming one who has quit and stayed.

There is enough psychological research to prove, that people still buy from people they like. Being honest, genuine and authentic does pay dividends.

Exercise:

What % would your team score you on being Authentic? _____%

Everything You Need To Learn About Leadership You Can Learn From A P1NEAPPLE

A survey of 733 millionaires listed their top two characteristics they feel helped them to be successful. The number one characteristic that they all agreed on was being *honest*. The second characteristic was to *always learn something new.*

🍍**And that is the L in VALUE, to learn.** People genuinely want to learn something new. Sometimes they are a little bit frightened of doing so, other times it is because they do not have that inner confidence. Our job, as a leader, is to help them develop that confidence and that sense of mastery.

That sense of being better today than we were yesterday to develop that sense of flow. An experience so enjoyable, that the people will do it, even at great cost, for the sheer sake of doing it. Imagine everyone in the team that you work with, having that same mentality.

The number one reason people leave a job is because they do not feel valued. So when we become stagnant, it's no wonder that we find so many people have switched off within six months of joining a company.

A few years ago, I had the privilege of working in a young offender's institute, trying to help the young people to get their lives back in order and see that there was a better way for them to go through the rest of their life. Every Wednesday morning, one of my jobs was to take half a dozen young men down to the library, where they had fifteen minutes in order to choose some books. The first time I went with them, I asked a young man, who had six books in his hand, which books he was going to get that day and about the books that he would normally read. He went on to tell me how he would read those 6 books within the week and that usually he would try different subjects.

The following week, I was again walking down to the library but this time with a different young man and I noticed that he had no books.

In fact, he had his hands in his pockets. I asked him what books he was going to get from the library and he replied that he would not be getting any. I asked him if he realised that it would be his only chance at the library that week and that he would not be able to come back to get any. His response was that he knew that. Puzzled, I pressed him further asking what he intended to do and he replied that he would not be getting any books from the library.

My brain was doing somersaults. I could not comprehend being locked up in a cell with nothing to read or do other than recline on my bunk bed; in which case, I was either looking at the mattress above me or at the ceiling for anywhere up to sixteen hours a day. I asked him, "What do you do when you are in your cell?" He looked at me as if I were from a different planet and said, "I don't do anything." From talking to him it became clear his reason for not reading was his lack of self-confidence and his need to defend his poor self-image. Most people want to learn, they want to get better. Better today than they were yesterday. I find it very difficult and saddening that there are still people in the world just like that young man; who want to learn and want to change where he was but his lack of self-confidence kept him a prisoner. Thankfully, the majority of people and the people who we work with will want to be able to be better today than yesterday.

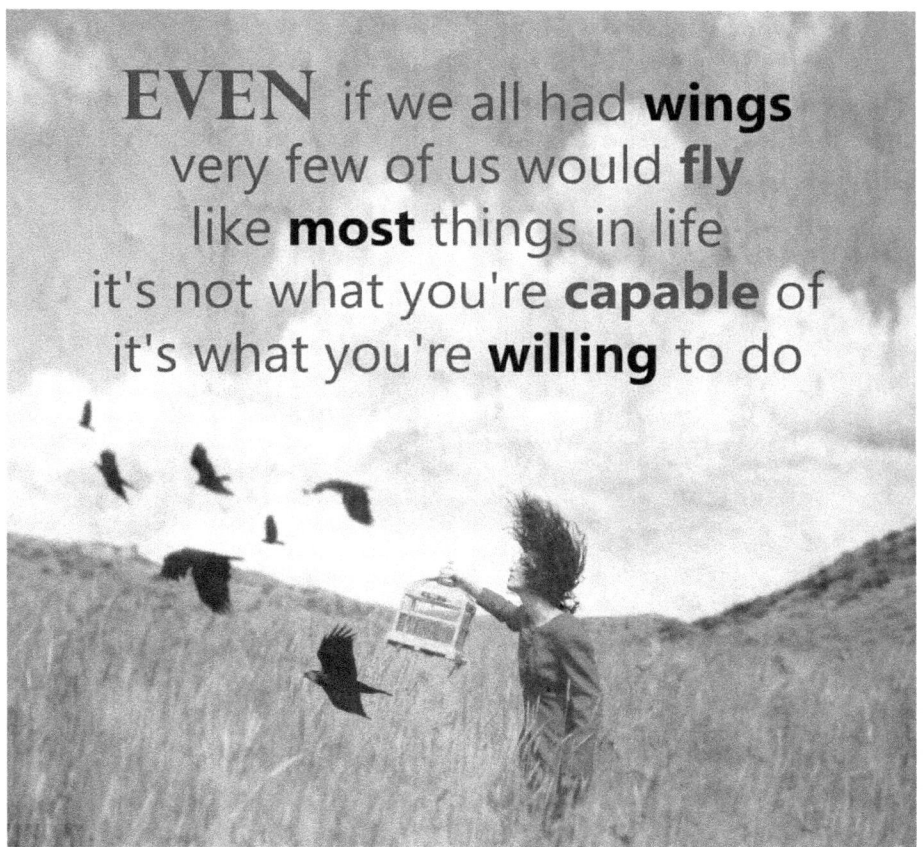

🍍 **The U in VALUE is for understand.** When we can understand something, we can put it into action. I may have the knowledge, but still I do not understand how to use it. Hence, transforming knowledge into positive action, transforming it into a direction we want to go; that is constructive, positive and dedicated practice. When people understand, they will know "why to" and then they want to know "how to". We need desperately to help people to not just have information but also to understand how to use it.

In his wonderful book "Gung Ho!", Ken Blanchard talks about the spirit of the squirrel and the power of worthwhile work. Everything we do should have that feeling of being worthwhile. When people fully understand they can get so involved in the activity that nothing else can distract them.

I would like to share with you two pieces of poetry that have had a massive impact in my life, but also that make me realize how important the U in VALUE is in relation to others and to ourselves.

The first is by my mentor Jim Rohn, described as one of the worlds foremost personal development teachers.

The Challenge
by Jim Rohn

Let others lead small lives,
But not you.
Let others argue over small things,
But not you.
Let others cry over small hurts,
But not you.
Let others leave their future in someone else's hands,
But not you.

Watch
by Frank Outlaw

Watch your thoughts, for they become words.
Watch your words, for they become actions.
Watch your actions, for they become habits.
Watch your habits, for they become character.
Watch your character, for it becomes your destiny.

How true both of these works are; these are powerful words to live your life by.

❖ The E in VALUE, is to have empathy. You see, *"people will never remember everything you said or everything you did, but they will always remember how you made them feel".*

How we are made to feel, will determine if we go that extra mile or if we stand side by side and share the load in support of each other. If we have that feeling of empathy with another human being, it takes us back to having a sense of belonging.

In my live seminars I go through a little experiment where we throw a little ball around between 3 people. At any given point, I ask two of them to exclude the other and not throw the ball to that person.

The reason I do this is because neuroscientists have now proven that if we are excluded, if we are shunned by people, it records in the same centre of the brain that physical pain records. So if we do not have that empathy, we do not allow people to have a voice, to be authentic, to learn and to understand, we are actually causing them a great physical pain. As I said before, people will never remember everything you did, people will never remember everything that you said, but they will always remember, how you made them feel.

When we put everything together remember, we are not paid for time, we are paid for adding value. In this resource driven world, more and more people feel that they are just a cog in a machine. The truth is that talented people do not go to work just to perform tasks, they want to offer ideas that can be discussed freely, honestly, and respectfully. They not only want to grow professionally, they want to feel that they contribute to the future success of the company. They want to be able to adapt to the present and to shape the future, faster, easier and better than their competitors. Our job is to help them to achieve that.

Change Management

One of the important aspects of understanding both BLADE and Change Management is to understand that the brain has a natural default position. When left to its own devices, the brain reverts back to chaos. When I am presenting in live seminars I normally take a wooden block game called Jenga and I tip the contents out to demonstrate that natural default position because when the blocks hit the floor, they just go into a state of chaos. The brain likes to have processes and structures; it needs to understand a plan and the reasons why, and understanding the five hard wire drives is a great step towards bringing that process, structure and plan.

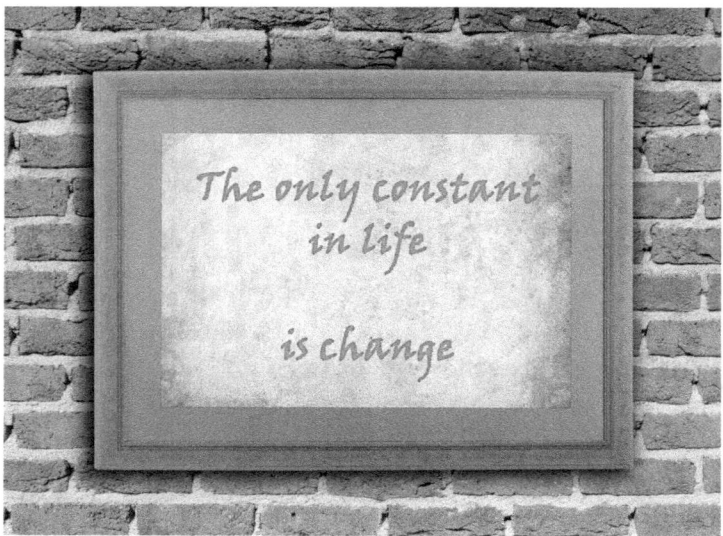

In the live seminars, I normally use the Jenga pieces to build a wall to show how important structure, process and planning are. It's the very reason why one of the worst punishments that can be administered without taking somebody's life is solitary confinement. When we leave people in solitary confinement with no sensory input, no night or day or means of telling the passing of time, the mind goes into a free fall causing the mind to remain in a state of chaos.

I would encourage you as a manager, as a leader, to begin to understand and make notes on each one of the people that you lead. What is it that they exhibit in their behaviour of the five hard wired drives the most? Understanding people more in order to help them to develop is vital to our success. In the research, 1233 of the most successful people agreed that they have a process, a structure and a plan that's clearly defined because they know how to harness the power of the mind.

Later, I will share with you the top five characteristics of successful managers and we will look at certain aspects of how we can learn from those benefits of understanding the top five characteristics, how we can develop them within ourselves and in those we manage and lead.

In Psychology we refer to the Gestalt cycle, a process and structure that the brain goes through outside of our awareness. There's a little part of the brain the hippocampus, that alert us to say, for example, that I'm thirsty and it's time to make a drink.

Another part of the cycle now forms in which to make a choice. So is it tea, coffee, a glass of lemonade or some water? Then having made a choice, I can go into action. I can go and get myself the drink that I have chosen to have. For some people, the choice section of the process is skipped and they go straight into action, which is great if their action is positive, but not so if their action is negative. These are the people that have those knee jerk reactions we often observe. They react rather than because they've missed out making the proper choice.

Having made a healthy, positive choice I then move on in the cycle to make contact and so I'll go get myself the drink. Once Ive had it, if I feel satisfied it switches off that little part of my brain that first alerted me to the fact that I wanted to take a drink. If there is no satisfaction, I'd revert back to choice and think well maybe the cup of tea that I've just had didn't quench my thirst, so I need something else.

When there's no satisfaction, when I can't complete that cycle, then what I'm left with is frustration. The more times I don't complete that cycle, the more I feel frustrated and the less chance there is that I will want to do it differently next time. So our job as leaders is to try and explain the process, the structure, but more importantly, the why. Simply explain that the reason they don't feel satisfied is probably because there are other unexplored choices out there, maybe it was a cool drink that was need rather than a hot one. As a leader, try to create that deeper understanding in order for their Gestalt cycle to be completed in a successful and rewarding way.

When you've done something and it's been successful and rewarding; you will want to do that over and over again. In Psychology, it's called the Law of Consistency. We will want to be consistent and perform to that level constantly, because we want to have that rewarding feeling repeatedly and be the best we can be.

Every time that I present a seminar, there's one person listening more intently than anyone else, that person is me; because I understand the law of consistency. The more I hear about structure, process and the plans for the brain, the more I understand why I need to make changes and the easier it is for me to change, to get it right the first time, because I don't want to redo, resend and refund.

I really would encourage you to be able to take on board all of the things we are saying, spend some time now to make some notes, do a little bit of reflection on how you can get people to belong. What is it you need to do in order to help them to learn?

What is it they need to acquire? Whether its skills, knowledge, confidence. Do they just need to know that it's okay to try and not always be

Everything You Need To Learn About Leadership You Can Learn From A P1NEAPPLE

successful? If they're stuck in a defence mode, they'll never give you that great idea. They'll never go that extra mile, they'll never step into that cigar tube to go half a mile underground to bring some great new idea to the surface and sadly they won't get the emotional connection.

› What is it you need to do in order to help them to learn?

› What is it they need to acquire? is it:

› Skills based?

› Knowledge based?

› Self-Confidence?

✓ Do they just need to know that it's okay to try and not always be successful first time?

If they're stuck in a defence mode, they'll never give you that great idea. They'll never go that extra mile, they'll never step into that cigar tube to go half a mile underground to bring some great new idea to the surface and sadly they won't get the emotional connection they are seeking.

When I leave people I want to leave them feeling better than when I first met them. I want to leave them with that hope that they can be better today than yesterday.

I spoke recently at a company and after the end of our first session I asked one of their Senior Executives two questions. Had it been worth his time? He said without a doubt. I then asked him what he was going to take away from the session and he said he needed to go and think about everything I had said, but that he would get back to me on it. A few days later he sent me an email, and he said the only way he could describe the session was that **"it was very profound and made such a difference to his life, his career"**. That's the beauty when people can connect to the information, and they can spend a little time reflecting. I said before, it takes twenty-four months for a pineapple to fully develop; all these pieces of information, I'd like you to see them almost as little seeds being planted in that fertile soil of your mind. Some seeds will germinate quickly, others will take a bit of nurturing; but it's that nurturing that helps them to fully develop to make those profound changes. Spend some time now just reflecting on where you are in terms of your ability to learn and belong, to have that emotional connection, to be able to acquire both material and non-material things and to defend yourself, your reputation and who you are. Always remember the minds' natural default position is chaos and the way out of chaos is process, structure and plan. One of the greatest bands of all time was the Beatles. One of the Beatles, George Harrison, wrote a song and the title of that song is "If you don't know where you're going, any road will take you there."

Please spend some time now thinking about what processes and structures you need to implement, what's the plan and why is it so important for you to achieve that goal that you're setting for yourself.

Please spend some time now thinking about what processes and structures you need to implement, what's the plan and why is it so important for you to achieve that goal that you're setting for yourself.

What changes do I need to make?

What is my plan to achieve those changes?

What structures do I need to implement to achieve this goal?

What are the processed needed in order for us to achieve the goal?

| |
| |
| |
| |

There is fascinating research I would like to share with you regarding achieving your goals in life:

The four main reasons people do not achieve their goals, they are:

1. No written goal,

2. No plan of action to achieve their goal,

3. Lack of self-confidence / self-belief,

4. Distracted from their goal by outside forces.

The success of achieving our goals:

Research has shown the difference in goal achievement; the control group results are as follows:

1. With no Written Goals, only 43% accomplished their goal,

2. Those who had Written Goals, 64% accomplished their goals,

3. Those who shared their goals with a trusted person a staggering 76% accomplished their goal.

PROBLEM 1:
No written goal: causing only 43% to accomplish their goal.

SOLUTION:
When left to its own devices the human brain has a natural default position: CHAOS. The brain loves structure, process and patterns. No goals, no process, no patterns and no structure results in varying levels of chaos.

The mind-set system taught in the leadership programme has been tried tested and proven by 1233 of the world's most successful business leaders.

PROBLEM 2:
No plan of action to achieve their goal.

SOLUTION:
This book is an introduction in taking control of your career and achieving more. The mentoring program will take you on a step-by-step journey all the way through the six laws of the mind that will enable you to make life changing decisions, but more importantly to be able to master them so that you can be happy in your career / life more easily, more often with less stress, less hassle and less frustration.

Structure and process, as we have established, are vital to the success of any organisation; so why would the mind be any different? Writing our goals focuses the mind into achieving more. 64% of those who have written goals accomplished them.

The reticular activating system of the brain is activated by three main elements: Authority, Intensity and Repetition. Repetition is where the mentoring programme scores highly; the use of regular meetings with managers holds them accountable for their actions wither they be positive or negative actions.

PROBLEM 3:
Lack of self-confidence / self-belief.

SOLUTION:
"You cannot consistently outperform the image you have of yourself".

We are less likely to ask for help or advice if our self-confidence or self-esteem is low. Increasing a person's self- confidence will foster the ability to share goals with a trusted person and the results state that when they shared them, 76% accomplished their goal.

This research highlights the benefit of having a clearly defined goal and purpose along with having a trusted person to help and support their desired outcome. Being able to share goals is determined by that person's level of self-confidence and self-belief.

By understanding your self-image and by learning to modify it and manage it to suit your purposes, you gain incredible confidence, personal power and self-belief.

The self-image controls what you can and cannot accomplish; what is difficult or easy for you, even how others respond to you. Just as certainly and scientifically as a thermostat controls the temperature in your home. Understanding and implementing the psychology of the self-image is the difference between success and failure in leadership.

Discovering your leadership self-image will rescue or prevent a faltering and crumbling career.

86% of successful managers confirm that:

"You Cannot Lead The Cavalry Charge If You Think You Look Silly On A Horse!".

The leadership mastery system takes managers and leaders on a journey that will guarantee them the self-image that will enable them to lead the cavalry with or without a horse!

Those with a written goal also indicated that by sharing it, they had to think more about how they would achieve it. This resulted in having a plan they could discuss and use to correct their course in order to achieve their desired outcome.

We can avoid falling back into old pathways by taking notice of some phenomenal psychological research by Professor Hermann Ebbinghaus. He discovered that if people don't fully connect with the information that they are given, they retain very little of it, and it would taper off very quickly.

In the psychology of leadership mastery mentoring program, we first of all ensure that people fully connect to the material and then we bring in interventions on a regular basis that prevent them from falling back into old pathways.

The mind operates very similarly to a cybernetic process. Just as a plane flying from England to New York never flies in a direct line, but is constantly adjusting its course and integrating new feedback in order for it to reach its desired destination, so the human mind also needs adjusting regularly to stay focused on goals. Once we program the mind and program the reticular activating system, it will want to constantly adjust our course, by integrating the feedback we receive, in order for us to achieve our goal.

Ebbinghaus curve

Professor Hermann Ebbinghaus conducted a series of experiments related to how we learn and retain information, his results are widely accepted as a general theory for how we learn and retain information.

Graphing his results, he developed a formula for how long items remain in our memory. Some people may remember better than others, but the general trend for how long we retain information is the same.

The resulting graph is called the **Ebbinghaus' Forgetting Curve.** The bad news is that it's steeper than you may think. The good news is that there are strategies you can use to improve your chance of retention.

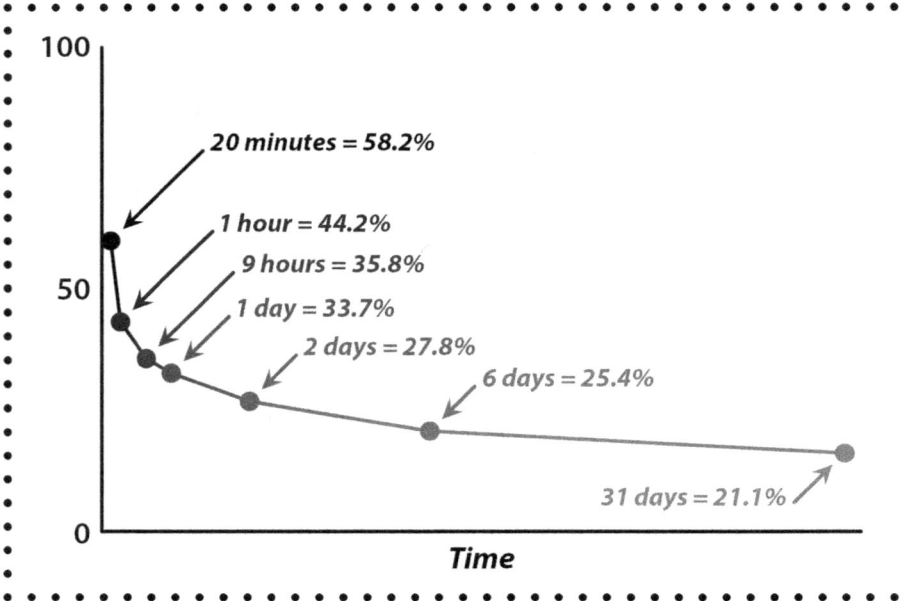

Everything You Need To Learn About Leadership You Can Learn From A P1NEAPPLE

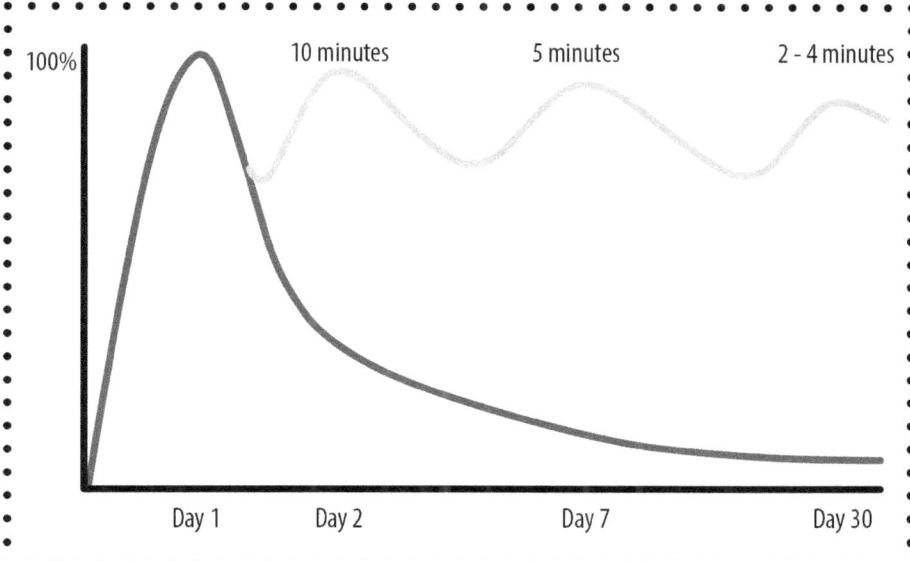

Participants who spend **10 minutes reviewing information within 24 hours of receiving will raise the curve almost to 100% again**.

A week later, it only takes 5 minutes to "reactivate" the same material and again raise the curve. By day 30, your brain will only need 2-4 minutes to give you the feedback, "Yes, I know that."

So how do we help them overcome the Ebbinghaus Curve? Well the speed of forgetting depends on a number of factors such as the meaningfulness of the information, stress level, repetition of information and the use of whole brain learning.

A better approach for long term retention is to focus on the quality of the information presented to us and the meaning of the information to you. If you learn something that it is important to you and you can connect it with many things you already know, your memory retention will be very high. The converse is also true.

This is why change is rarely permanent and will evaporate over time. It is easy to forget if we do nothing to fix it in the mind.

The Psychology of Leadership Mastery is founded on the principle of understanding both the mind and our behaviour in order to create lasting positive change.

MOTIVATION and MOMENTUM

There are two forms of motivation: intrinsic and extrinsic. Intrinsic and extrinsic types of motivation have been widely studied. The distinction between them has shed important light on how leaders can develop the teams that they lead.

But let us first have a look at the definition of being motivated. To be motivated means: to be moved to do something. A person, who feels no desire or purpose to act, is thus classed as unmotivated; where as someone who is energized, involved and active towards an end result, is considered motivated.

Intrinsic motivation is defined as: doing an activity for the sheer pleasure and satisfaction of doing it, rather than, some external reward or punishment. When intrinsically motivated, a person is moved to act, for the sheer fun and pleasure that simple challenge entails rather than because of an external pressure, reward, or punishment. The phenomenon of intrinsic motivation was first acknowledged back in 1959; where it was discovered that many people engage in curiosity driven types of behaviours, even in the absences of reinforcement, reward or punishment.

These behaviours appear to be not done for any such instrumental reason, but rather the positive experiences associated with experiencing and expanding our capability. Similar to what we have motioned before about mastery. If it leads us to being better today than we are yesterday, then intrinsic motivation has a great deal of traction.

From our very birth and onwards, as human beings, we are actively inquisitive, curious and, in some cases, playful creatures. Displaying an all too readiness to learn and explore. As with most babies, they do not require an incentive to do so.

So again, this is one of our hard-wire drives that we have spoken about; the desire to learn and acquire new things. This natural motivational tendency is a critical element in leadership development. It is through acting on one's inherent interest that one grows both in knowledge and skill.

Intrinsic motivation exists in the relationship between the individuals, and the activity. People are intrinsically motivated for some activities, and not others. Not everyone is intrinsically motivated for any particular task. However, because intrinsic motivation exists between a person and a task, some researchers have defined intrinsic motivation in terms of the task, while others have defined it in terms of the satisfaction a person gains while engaged in intrinsically motivated tasks.

There are two ways in which we can intrinsically motivate individuals. The first is to understand the basic principles of motivation. There are three basic ingredients in helping people to become more motivated.

I am going to use the acronym of **MAP.**

M as we have already discovered, is about mastery. If people feel that need, that desire and purpose to embrace a task, because they themselves will feel that sense of mastery, then their motivation is already ignited. A feeling of mastery comes when people set out on a challenge. There are always people who know the answer to their challenge of how they are going to succeed. It is the sheer excitement and understanding that this is something new and challenging that helps them to develop that sense of mastery.

The **A** stands for autonomy. People do not want to be micromanaged. They do not need to be given a job and then told precisely every little detail of how to complete that task. What they need is that ability to develop that skill. Guidance is often quite important within that, but it is allowing people to explore and expand and get involved in the task, rather than having it dictated to them. A sense of autonomy is quite important, when we are looking to develop and create that wonderful sense of intrinsic motivation.

The **P** stands for purpose. If we can see the bigger picture, if we can see the purpose of why we are doing the task at hand, then our instant ability to switch on that intrinsic motivation lies deep within us. All we have to do is connect preferably to all three of these points: Mastery, Autonomy and Purpose. Once a person begins to understand their purpose, and its bigger commitment to the wider picture, they can begin quite easily to develop a sense of motivation.

When we look at the different aspects of motivation, some people are simply motivated by money while some people are motivated by the challenge. In order to develop that intrinsic motivation, it is the challenge, the fun and excitement, that we are looking to develop.

If people are rewarded by money, for example, that is classed as extrinsic motivation. That means there is an external force, a drive outside of the human, that allows them to be driven forward. Now there is nothing wrong with having extrinsic motivation, if we are looking to create that deep meaning of flow where we are doing a task just for the fun, and the excitement of doing it. We will be far more committed, far more willing to go that extra mile, to complete the task. It is quite important for us, to understand the basics of motivation. In particular having generated motivation, our task now is to keep the momentum flowing. I referred earlier, how to use the Newton's cradle idea. That energy is self-generating if it is intrinsic, rather than extrinsic. All energy that is self-generating is far less stressful on the manager or leader, than having to constantly go out there and try to fire up the people so that they can be involved, inspired and ignited.

We discussed earlier the four reasons people do not achieve their goals. In relation to momentum and motivation, research confirms that the four main reasons people do not achieve their goals, and they are as follows.

GOALS

1. _____
2. _____
3. _____
4. _____

1. They have no written goal,

2. No plan of action to achieve their goal,

3. A lack of self-confidence or self-belief,

4. They are distracted from their goal by outside forces.

Let's now explore these four points in more detail:

It's been measured in the brain that if we externalise goals by writing them down, it has a more powerful effect on us. It's a form of validation that makes a statement to the world.

When we write our goals, it's quite important that we write them out in the present tense as if we have already achieved those goals, rather than have them in future tense. It's not particularly helpful to say 'I will be' as appose to saying 'I am now'.

It's all well and good to have a written goal, but it is only part of the plan, because without a plan of action it's very difficult for us to achieve. Remember the Japanese proverb that says 'A vision without action is a daydream; action without vision is a nightmare.'

Having a plan also needs to have structure and process. The brain prefers to have structure and process rather than being left to its own devices.

A lack of self-confidence and self-belief relates to the research findings of Dr Joyce Brothers that 'We cannot consistently outperform the image we have of ourselves.'

In the years that I have been teaching the psychology of leadership mastery, I have used an emotional intelligence profile that measures both self-esteem and self-confidence. There's a very strong correlation between a person having a low self confidence and self-esteem and their ability to set a goal and more importantly set out on the path to achieve it.

You can see by the two radar graphs below.

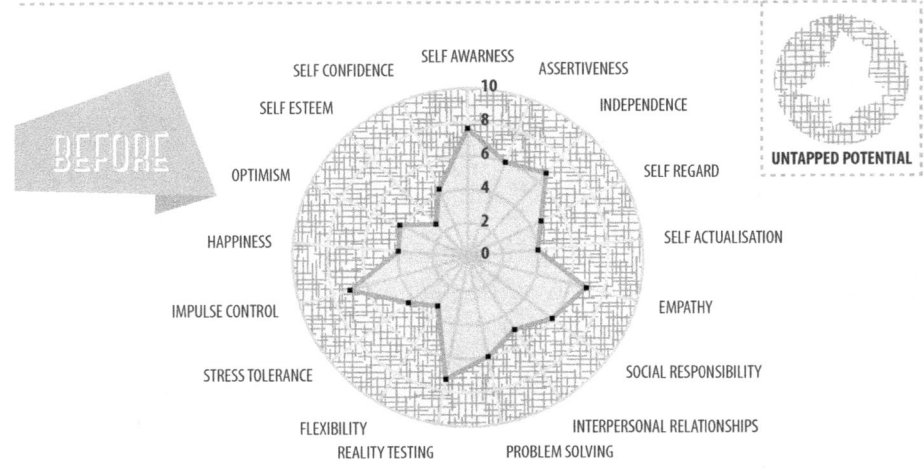

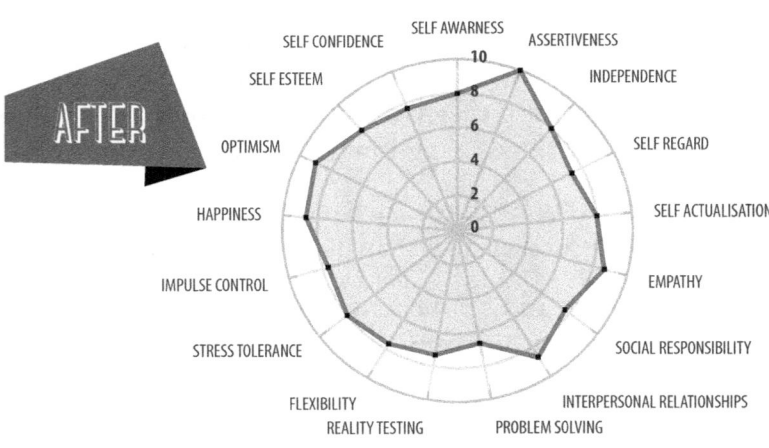

Leadership Mastery Orientation System

These are genuine graphs of before and after the profile was taken. If you'd like to take the profile for free please e-mail me at:

john@thepineappleman.co.uk

It will take you approximately 10 min to complete. I'll send you the profile, and then you and I can have a conversation and I will be able to explain the results of the profile.

The fourth reason people don't achieve their goals is being distracted from the goal by outside forces that we sometimes have no control over.

Stephen Covey in his book the Seven Habits of Highly Successful People talks about controlling the controllable to ensure that outside forces do not distract us.

Take as much action as you can in order to eliminate distractions. I rent office space with no Wi-Fi and no phone simply to have a space to think, process and to be creative.

Take as much action as you can in order to eliminate distractions. I rent office space with no Wi-Fi and no phone simply to have a space to think, process and to be creative.

I would recommend that you continue reading the remaining chapters and then visit the bonus chapter titled: Great by Choice Goal Setting Workbook starting on page 131.

The 17 Competencies that Underpin Leadership Mastery

Dr. Daniel Goleman, Psychologist, author of "Emotional Intelligence; Why It Matters More Than IQ" states:

"If your emotional abilities aren't in hand, if you don't have self-awareness, if you are not able to manage your distressing emotions, if you can't have empathy and have effective relationships, then no matter how smart you are, you are not going to get very far".

Emotional intelligence is four times more important when predicting one's success than IQ. The reason that this is so significant is we can move our IQ perhaps by a few points; but we can expand our EQ much more significantly. Becoming aware of the competencies that underpin EQ and leadership mastery allows us to develop and strengthen our skills as a leader.

Dr. Reuven Bar-On, a pioneer in the field of emotional intelligence, developed the EQ-I Bar-On Emotional Quotient Inventory. It measures 5 categories with 15 total competencies. However, I have added two extra competences to the list based on working with hundreds of companies, where the research confirms a correlation between low self-esteem and our ability to set and achieve goals, known as Self-Actualisation.

The 17 core competencies are:
Intrapersonal:
- Assertiveness,
- Self-regard,
- Self-actualization,
- Independence,
- Emotional self-awareness.

Interpersonal:
- Interpersonal relationships,
- Social Responsibility,
- Empathy.

Adaptability:
- Problem-solving,
- Reality testing,
- Flexibility.

Stress Management:
- Impulse Control,
- Stress Tolerance,
- General Mood,
- Happiness,
- Optimism.

Self-Confidence and Self-Esteem

Focusing and developing these competencies is important for leaders because it corrals the power of the mind and emotions by beginning to tame its wide outbursts and inappropriate responses. When we engage with others we can quickly get into a place of reacting rather than responding. "You don't care what I or anyone else has to say – you never listen."That statement is very obviously a reaction and is likely to not be received well!

Your inability to control your impulse to react is quite disruptive. It takes away from others being able to contribute and engage in the conversation. More importantly for leaders it takes away from any powerful message that you want or need to deliver.

Leaders need to be aware of how they can influence their careers both positively and negatively when they become known for their outbursts and reactions to situations rather than their levelheaded responses. By understanding the competencies of emotional intelligence, we have the opportunity to increase our EQs. We can create new habits and change the way we approach situations. This will only improve our level of success in our work, and in our lives.

Imagine for a few seconds if every person in the company you own or work for had all of the following competencies. It would ensure that stress, hassle and frustration would be kept to minimum while we all achieved more success, more often and more easily.

In explaining the benefits of developing each of the competences, I will quote directly from the work of Dr. Steven Stein and Howard E. Book M.D. They list the 15 competencies in their excellent book that I strongly recommend you buy a copy entitled "The EQ Edge", while the definition of Self-Confidence and Self Esteem are my own, taken from a two year research project into Self-Esteem and Confidence.

The 17 core competencies
The 5 Components of the Intrapersonal Realm

•Assertiveness

Assertiveness is composed of three basic components:

1. The ability to express feelings openly. The ability to express beliefs and thoughts openly being able to voice opinions disagree and taking definitive stand even if it is emotionally difficult to sell and even if you have something to lose by doing so.

2. The ability to stand up for personal rights not allowing others to take advantage of us.

Assertive people are not shy they're able to express their feelings and beliefs and they can do so without being aggressive or abusive.

•Self-regard

The ability to respect and accept yourself as basically good and respecting yourself is essentially, liking the way you are.

Self-regard is the ability to appreciate your perceived positive aspects possibilities as well as to accept your negative aspects and limitations and still feel good about you.

It's knowing your strengths and weaknesses, and liking yourself, warts and all.

This conceptual component of emotional intelligence is associated with general feelings of security, inner strength, self-assuredness, and self-confidence and feelings of self-adequacy.

Because individuals with healthy self-regard know their strengths and weaknesses, they feel good about themselves. They have no trouble openly and appropriately acknowledging when they have made mistakes or are wrong or don't know all the answers.

Feeling sure of oneself is dependent upon self-respect and self-esteem, which are based on a fairly well-developed sense of identity. People with good self-regard are fulfilled and satisfied with themselves.

•Self-actualization

This is the ability to realise your potential capacity. This component of emotional intelligence is manifested by becoming involved in pursuits that lead to a meaningful, rich and full life. Striving to actualise your potential involves developing enjoyable and meaningful activities and can mean a lifelong effort and an enthusiastic commitment to long-term goals.

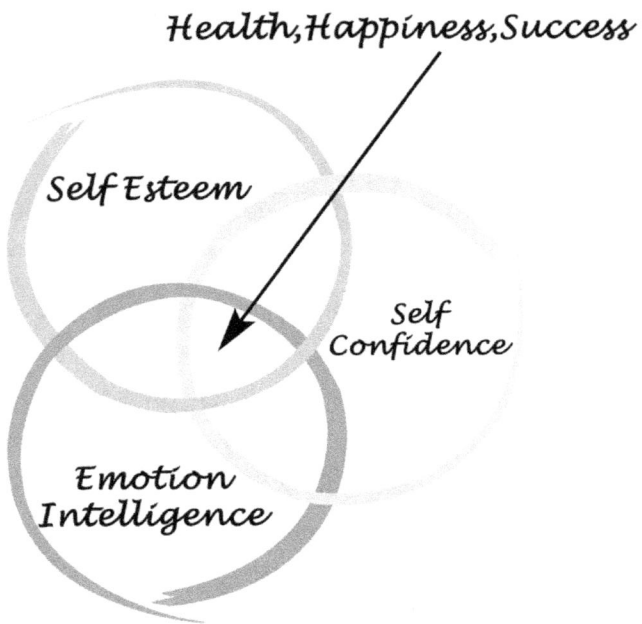

Self-actualisation is an ongoing, dynamic process of striving towards the maximum development of your abilities and talents, persistently trying to do your best and to improve yourself in general.

Excitement about your interests energises and motivates you to continue with them. Self-actualisation is affiliated with feelings of self-satisfaction.

Individuals with healthy self-actualisation are pleased with the location they find themselves at on life's highway with respect to their personal occupational and financial destinations.

•Independence

The ability to be self-directed and self-controlled in your thinking and actions and to be free of emotional dependence.

Independent people are self-reliant in planning and making important decisions. They can stand on their own two feet. They may, however seek and consider other people's opinions before making the right decisions for themselves in the end; consulting others is not necessarily a sign of dependency.

Independent people are able to function autonomously; they avoid clinging to others in order to satisfy their emotional needs. The ability to be independent rests on one's degree of self-confidence and industry, and the desire to meet expectations and obligations without becoming a slave to them.

•Emotional self-awareness

The ability to recognise your feelings, to differentiate between them, and identify why you are feeling them and to recognise the impact feelings have on others around you.

The 3 Components of the Interpersonal Realm:

•Interpersonal relationships

This is the ability to establish and maintain mutually satisfying relationships that are characterised by intimacy and by giving and receiving affection.

Having mutual satisfaction and meaningful social interchanges that are potentially rewarding and enjoyable, characterised by give and take.

Positive interpersonal relationship skills are characterised by sensitivity towards others. This component of emotional intelligence is not only associated with the desire to cultivate friendly relationships with others, but with the ability to feel at ease and comfortable in such relationships and to possess positive expectations concerning social interactions.

•Social Responsibility

This is the ability to demonstrate that you are a cooperative, contributing and constructive member of your social group.

This component of emotional intelligence involves acting in a responsible manner, even though you might not benefit personally. To do things for and with others, accept others, acting in accordance with your conscience and upholding social rules.

Socially responsible people have social consequences and basic concern for others, which is manifested by being able to take on community orientated responsibilities. They possess interpersonal sensitivity and are able to accept offers and use their talents of good of the collective, not just the self.

People who are deficient in this ability often entertain antisocial attitudes, act abusively towards others and take advantage of them.

It's doing something for the team, the division and the organisation and for society at large that does not benefit you directly.

•Empathy

The ability to be aware of, to understand and appreciate your thoughts on others. Empathy is tuning in, being sensitive to how and why people feel the way they do. It means being able to emotionally read other people. Empathic people care about others and show interest in and concern for them.

It is the ability to non-judgementally put into words your understanding of the other person's perspective on the world, even if you do not agree with it, even if you find that prospective ridiculous.

Being empathic shifts an adversarial relationship to a collaborative relationship.

The 3 Components of the Adaptability Realm:

•Problem-solving

The ability to identify and define problems as well as to generate and implement potential effective solutions.

Problem solving is multiphasic in nature and includes the ability to go through a process of:

1. Sensing the problem and feeling confident and motivated to deal with the problem effectively.

2. Defining and formulating the problem as clearly as possible. (gather relevant information).

3. Generating as many solutions as possible. (brainstorming).

4. Making a decision to implement which of the solutions having weighed the pros and cons of each possible solution and choosing the best course of action.

5. Assessing the outcome of the implemented solution.

6. Repeating this process if the problem still exists, being conscientious, disciplined, methodical and systematic in persevering and approaching problems.

This skill is also linked to a desire to do one's best and to confront problems, rather than avoid them.

•Reality testing

The ability to assess the correspondence about what is being experienced and to more objectively exist. Reality testing involves tuning in to the immediate situation. The best simple sentence definition of reality testing is that it is the capacity to see things objectively, the way they are, rather than the way we wish or fear them to be.

Testing this involves a search for objective evidence to confirm, justify and support feelings, perceptions and thoughts. The emphasis is on the pragmatism, the adequacy of your perception and authentication of your ideas and thoughts.

An important aspect of this component involves the ability to concentrate and focus when trying to access them and cope with situations that arise.

Reality testing is associated with a lack of withdrawal from the outside world, a tuning into the immediate situation and lucidity and clarity in perception and thought processes.

In simple terms, reality testing is the ability to accurately size up the immediate situation.

•Flexibility

The ability to adjust your emotions, thoughts and behaviour to changing situations and conditions.

This component of emotional intelligence applies to your overall ability to adapt to unfamiliar, unpredictable and dynamic circumstances. Flexible people are actually the synergistic ones and are capable of reacting to change without rigidity.

These people are able to change their minds when evidence suggests that they are mistaken. They are generally open and tolerant to different ideas, orientations, ways and practices. Their capacity to shift thoughts and behaviours is not arbitrary or whimsical, but rather in concert with shifting feedback that they are getting from their environment.

Individuals who lack the capacity are tangibly rigid and obstinate, they adapt poorly to new situations and have little capacity to take advantage of new opportunities.

The 2 Components of the Stress Management Realm:

•Impulse Control

The ability to resist and delay an impulse, drive or temptation to act. Impulse control entails a capacity for identifying your anger and aggressive impulses, being composed and putting the brakes on anger, aggressive, hostile and irresponsible behaviour.

Problems in impulse control has manifested a low frustration tolerance, impulsiveness, anger control problems, abusiveness, loss of self-control and explosive and unpredictable behaviour.

Impulsive people have often been described as tempestuous, hot-headed, and leap before they look.

•Stress Tolerance

The ability to withstand adverse events in stressful situations without developing physical or emotional symptoms by actively and positively coping with stress.

This ability is based on:

1. A capacity to choose courses of action for dealing with stress, being resourceful and effective, being able to come up with suitable methods, knowing what to do and how to do it.

2. An optimistic disposition towards new experiences and change in general and towards your own ability to successfully overcome a specific problem at hand.

3. The feeling that you can control or influence the stressful situation by staying calm and maintaining control. Stress tolerance includes having a repertoire to handle stressful situations. It is associated with the capacity to be relaxed and composed and to calmly face difficulties without getting carried away by strong emotions.

People with good stress tolerances tend to face crises and problems rather than surrendering to feelings of helplessness and hopelessness.

Anxiety, which often results when this component is not functioning adequately, has an ill effect on the general performance because it contributes to poor concentration, difficulty in making decisions and somatic problems such as sleep disturbance.

The 2 Components of the General Mood Realm

•Happiness

The ability to feel satisfied with your life, to enjoy yourself and others and to have fun. Happiness combines self-satisfaction, general contentment and the ability to enjoy life.

Happy people often feel good and at ease in both work and leisure; they are able to let their hair down and enjoy the opportunities of having fun.

Happiness is associated with a general feeling of cheerfulness and enthusiasm. It is a by-product and the barometer of your overall degree of emotional intelligence and emotional functioning.

The person who demonstrate a low degree of this competent may possess symptoms of depression, such as a tendency to worry, uncertainty about the future, social withdrawal, lack of drive, depressive thoughts, feelings of guilt, dissatisfaction with life and their job.

•Optimism

The ability to look at the brighter side of life and to maintain a positive attitude, even in the face of adversity, optimism assumes a measure of hope in one's approach to life. It is a positive approach to daily living. Optimism is the opposite of pessimism, which is a common symptom of depression.

Self-Confidence

Here is a dictionary definition of confidence that I have added to based on my research. Once again I would ask you to imagine all of the people you work with displaying these areas of self-confidence;

CONFIDENCE (noun).

the noun CONFIDENCE has 4 senses:

1. Freedom from doubt; belief in yourself and your abilities,

2. A feeling of trust in someone or something,

3. A state of confident hopefulness that events will be favourable,

4. A trustful relationship,

Lets look at the four points in more detail.

1. Freedom of doubt: belief in yourself and your abilities:

How many times in your life have you either talked yourself out of doing something you later regret?

When people develop their self-confidence they are excited about new projects, they become involved and inspired rather that fearful and withdrawn from the project.

2. A feeling of trust in someone or something:

Think back to the Chilean president and the Pakistani president who would you put your trust in and more importantly who would you go that extra mile for.

People will be willing to lay down their lives for a person or situation they trust and believe in. I am thinking of the paramedic who got into the cigar tube to help rescue the 33 Chilean miners.

The great thing about self-confidence is when everybody has it, it becomes contagious. Jim Rohn famously said, "You are the average of the 5 people you spend the most time with." by increasing the average of those five people you automatically increase your average.

3. <u>A state of confident hopefulness that events will be favourable:</u>

Optimists contemplate if the glass as half full, pessimists contemplate if the glass as half empty, while they are contemplating a self-confident person would have drank the water. We are paid to add value not for our time; we need people around us who have a desire to see the task in hand in a favourable light.

4. <u>A trustful relationship:</u> go back to your list of character traits from the boss, manager your most respected, I have no doubt that you will agree that you had a trustful relationship with them.

Self-Esteem

I undertook a two year University validated research program to study self-esteem. I set out to identify the cause of poor self-esteem and more importantly how to develop self-esteem not only in ourselves, to then be able to teach it too others:

I have put together a collection of tried tested and proven ways to develop self-esteem to leaders, managers, parents and children. My definition of self-esteem is:

Self-Esteem is the favourable or unfavourable opinion and self-image we have of ourselves. It is this opinion and self-image that individuals strive to maintain. It is the maintenance of the self-image and opinion that will determine our levels of: self-confidence, self-respect, self-efficacy and self-worth therefore creating self-consistency within the individual as we cannot consistently outperform the image we have of ourselves.

Emotional intelligence like our IQ is not fixed; Professor Dweck refers to us as having incremental intelligence rather than it being fixed. The benefit of this is we can change any aspect of our personality or leadership style should we choose too.

Developing our ability to connect with people is without doubt a major factor in our success as a leader. I asked you in the beginning of this chapter to imagine for a few seconds if every person in the company you work with had all of these competencies and how it would ensure that stress, hassle and frustration would be kept to a minimum while we all achieved more success, more often and more easily. The good news is that we can change our leadership style for the better, we can teach the people skills needed to become the person people look up to no matter how tall they grow.

Take a few minutes to visit www.thepineappleman.co.uk and take the 10 minute evaluation of your emotional intelligence, self-esteem and self-confidence.

The Six Laws Of The Mind

I'd like to introduce to you the six laws of the mind. These laws allow us to take control of every aspect of our life.

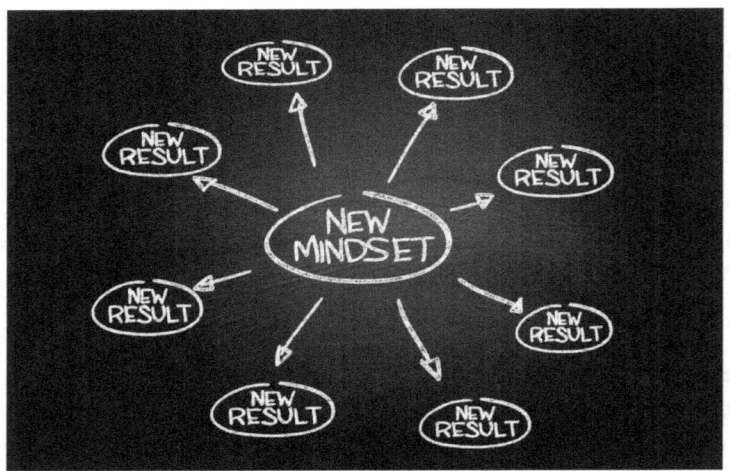

Understanding and working with the six laws will enable you to:

› Be able to harness and control the power of your subconscious mind,

› Develop your creativity,

› Improve your self-esteem,

› Change your self-image,

› Develop a mind-set that will help you achieve more success more often more easily.

It is vital to understand that our mind is never stationary, it is constantly moving, thinking, planning and as we discussed in earlier chapters, if left in its own devices the mind has a natural default position of chaos.

The six laws of the mind help prevent that chaos and they are techniques that you need practice daily in order to fully harness uncontrolled power of your mind.

The first law is that Thoughts Have Birth Certificates

What do I mean by thoughts have birth certificate? Whatever we pay attention to expands in the mind. Our mind doesn't care whether we are paying attention to positive or negative thoughts; our mind is simply going through the process.

Try this exercise; take a few seconds to sit with your eyes closed and hold in your mind a very positive thought. You could think of a loved one or a recent event that brings a smile to your face just thinking about it. While you holding the thought, notice on your body where you are feeling it.

Now what I want you to do is just be aware of that area that you're feeling this positive thought on your body and just keep holding the thought in your mind. Keep running the thought around as if it was on a video inside your head and what you will notice very quickly the positive feeling that you're experiencing on your body will begin to expand.

The mind will go through the same procedure whether the thought is negative or positive; it's a process that your mind runs with every thought. The important fact here is that we can control whether we are running a positive thought or a negative thought because whatever we pay attention to will expand.

Be careful what thought you are running in your mind.

Take sometime over the coming weeks to become the observer of your own thought, I would recommend that you keep a journal and note down all the positive and negative thoughts that you have been running. As I have said; thoughts have birth certificates and the mind doesn't care which one of them is positive or negative.

The Second Law of the Mind Is That:

The mind is a receiving station as we have discussed the mind is never still; it is constantly moving, thinking and processing. The mind receives over 2 million bits of information per second. It has to filter them in order for us to function and to pay attention to what our dominant thoughts are.

A perfect example of this filter system and receiving station would be that of a parent. During the evening, your mind can filter out noises such as the radiator ticking in the corner, any movement or creaking in the house in order to allow you to sleep, but should the baby cry or stir, you will instantly wake up and attend to the baby's needs.

Our mind is constantly receiving information that psychologists call outside awareness, this is where information is being picked up by our brain but we're not particularly paying any conscious attention to it. TV advertising, marketing and product placements on television and in films are a perfect example of how the mind receives information that is both in our awareness and outside of our awareness.

I recently spoke on BBC radio regarding the dangers of how we are affected by the information we receive outside of our conscious awareness.

The important factor here as a leader, manager or supervisor is to be aware that people receive and process information not only by watching us, they are also aware when our words don't match our actions. All of this is happening outside of our awareness, and as a result of their observations they will form an opinion as to how trusting, honest and reliable we are as leader's managers and supervisors.

We need to be constantly aware that other people will be reading, interpreting and analysing our actions, words, facial expressions and tone of voice. If we are trying to develop relationships and build rapport, so that those we manage will go the extra mile, we need to be in control of all these aspects to ensure that the message they receive is not only positive but builds trust and honesty; ensuring that we become the person people look up to no matter how tall they grow.

The third law of the mind is the law of attraction

We have discovered that thoughts have birth certificates and that the mind is a constant receiving station. We have also discussed the part that the reticular activating system plays in how successful we are at achieving our goals. It filters out anything that isn't important to us, allowing the law of attraction to take place.

Thoughts that are emotionalised become magnified and magnetised; any thought that we have significant emotion attached to, will become magnified. Those thoughts have birth certificates and whatever we pay attention to is heightened. The more emotional content our thoughts hold, the more the magnifications will increase. This then becomes a catch 22 process within the brain; the more emotionalised and magnified our thoughts become the more we attract those same things to us because our thoughts have now been magnetised.

The catch 22 part of this law is that the mind does not care whether the thoughts are positive or negative. We must be fully aware of the thoughts that we are allowing our mind to magnify and magnetise. If our thoughts are positive, goal orientated and take us in the direction we desire to going then happily let your mind attract to you all of the creativity, clarity and actions you need to take in order to achieve your goal. However, if we are allowing negative thoughts to be magnetised and magnified then we will attract more of that negativity. If we apply this law to leadership, it is vital that we ensure that our thoughts are focused on solutions to the problem not just the problem.

Because the mind is a receiving station, we need to convey to the people we manage and lead that we are solution focused not problem focused.

The fourth law of the mind is control the mind

We have covered this particular law in discussing the three previous laws where we have clearly stated that if left to its own devices the natural default position of the mind is chaos and that the mind loves structure, process and plans.

As leaders, we need to fully be aware that we may need to help those we manage to have more structure, process and plans. This will enable others to be more successful, more often, more easily and with less stress, less hassle and less frustration and avoid having to redo resend or refund; all of which directly affect both our career and the bottom line profit.

The fifth law of the mind is similar to a mathematical formula

Thoughts + Information + Understanding = Action.

Let me explain; let's assume that you moved house in a new area and you would like to join the library.

What is the information that you need to add to your thought in order to achieve your goal?

- You would need to know where the library is,
- You would need to know the opening and closing times,
- You would need to know what documentation you require to take in order to gain a library card.

Having information does not always lead to action because if we don't understand the information and we cannot integrate it into our awareness, then it inevitably will not lead to taking action.

I understand that if I turn up to the correct address, at the correct opening time and with the necessary documentation to prove my address, I am more likely to take the action required in order for me to receive my library card.

How does this apply to leadership mastery? If we are to examine some of the actions that the people we manage and lead take, we can see how by applying this formula we can begin to understand their thought processes. Maybe they need more information, or more understanding in order to be able to take positive action and change unwanted behaviours.

This is the most powerful tool. When understood and applied; it allows us to be very specific in the areas which need to change. If it is more information, then we can simply apply the information that is missing. If it is a deeper understanding or a clearer understanding, then again we can apply that which allows the person to gain that clearer understanding; all of which can then be applied to the positive new behaviour or action.

"John has given me the power and methodology to logically work through issues swiftly with positive outcomes". - Dean Jennings: Kongsberg Maritime Sales Manager Off Shore Production Systems UK and Ireland.

The sixth and final law of the mind is that our inner and outer worlds connect

We live in two simultaneous worlds. We live in a world inside our head and we live in the outer world; in this case we will this focus on our world inside work.

We all experience being in an environment which is intimidating, threatening or just uncomfortable and we know from past experience that being in this environment affects our thoughts and feelings.

As a manager, leader or supervisor it is vital that we understand how the inner and outer worlds connect. In the second law of the mind we experienced how our actions are being received by others and this again is a perfect example of where our inner and outer worlds connect.

If I am perceiving your actions, words, body language or demeanour to be intimidating, threatening or uncomfortable; I will be releasing a hormone called Cortisol which affects my ability to think clearly and make positive decisions as I will be more focused on defending than developing.

If I perceive your actions as open, accommodating and positive, I will naturally be releasing hormones that will aid my thinking and my clarity in liability to take positive action.

These six laws of the mind are an essential part of your toolkit as a leadership master, if you would like to know more about the six laws of the mind, I run a one-day workshop where we cover them in more depth allowing you to take the information, to understand it and more importantly; put it into positive action.

Creating FLOW and Goal Achievement

The control study we discussed earlier covers three areas.

1. In the control group when no written goals only 43% accomplish their goals.

2. Those who had written goals, 64% accomplished their goals.

3. Those who shared their goals with a trusted person, a staggering 76% accomplish their goals.

Problem one is that no written goal causes only 43% to accomplish their goal and the solution when left to its own devises, puts the brain in its natural default position which we've already said is chaos.

The brain loves structure, process and patterns. No goals, no process. No patterns and no structure will result in varying levels of chaos. So looking back at each individual member of your team: what are their written goals? When have you sat down with them? On an annual or six month basis? Have you set out a plan, a goal for them to be part of?

The first important element of creating that sense of flow, that generates intrinsic motivation, is that people need to be involved in their own goal setting.

The second most important area of creating a sense of flow is that the goal needs to be a stretch, but not too far. It needs to be achievable, but it has to create a stretch within them.

The third most important area of creating a sense of flow as a leader and manager is the quality and the regularity of the feedback which you give to the people you're working with. Feedback needs to be two things. It needs to be fairly instant, as soon after an event as possible.

Equally it needs to be very specific. The more specific you can be, the better it is and the easier for people to learn.

The solution to the problem of not having a plan of action to achieve their goal is to help people take control of their career and achieve more. This is one of the beauties of a mentoring program which takes you through a step by step journey through both the six laws of the mind and how to set a goal as well as the ability to achieve it. When you give feedback there are two main elements to consider: instant and specific.

Out of those who have written goals, 64% accomplish their goal. The reticular activating system of the brain is activated by three main elements: authority, intensity and repetition. So as a leader and manager, you already have the authority. If you have the skills and the background to be able to help somebody achieve their goal, then you naturally have the first element that the reticular activating systems of the brain requires, that feeling of authority.

Intensity is about that emotional connection. It's about how well we connect and how well we can help people to feel good and how we can help them to develop themselves to be better today than yesterday.

The fourth important component of FLOW is to create an emotional connection to the goal by linking it to their personal development

Repetition goes back to the element of dedicated practice. Rather than practicing your faults, it is about dedicated practice that is constructive and goal oriented.

Repetition is where mentoring programs score highly because the use of regular meetings with management holds them accountable for their actions, whether they are positive or negative actions, they need to be addressed.

The lack of self-confidence, self-esteem, and self-belief, are the main areas I work on to eliminate the following: 'You cannot consistently out-perform the image you have of yourself'.

We are less likely to ask for help if our self-confidence or self-esteem is low. Increasing a person's self-confidence will bring in the ability to share goals with a trusted person. The results prove this because 76% accomplished their goals when they shared them. This research highlights the benefits of having a clearly defined goal and purpose, along with having a trusted person to help and support their desired outcome. Being able to share goals is determined by that person's level of self-confidence and self-belief.

Following on the work of Professor Bandura and Dr. Brothers, the statement: 'You cannot consistently outperform the image you have of yourself' reflects a person's ability to share their desired outcome and then to set out on the journey to achieve their goals.

I make no apology for repeating this because it's one of the most important areas of leadership that we need to understand and develop. By understanding your self-image and by learning to modify and manage it to suit your purposes, you gain incredible confidence, personal power and self-belief.

The self-image controls what you can do and what you do not accomplish. What is difficult or easy for you, even how others respond to you. Just as certainly and as scientifically as a thermostat controls the temperature in the room, your self-image will control your level of success. Understanding and implementing the psychology of the self-image is the difference between success and failure in leadership.

As an example, when I go into a company, and I'm working with their senior management team, the most common problem that I face is working with somebody who sees themselves perhaps as a very good engineer, but then feels totally de-skilled when they are promoted. They are promoted for their product knowledge but not for their people skills, and that massively affects their self-image, but more importantly, it massively effects how they interact with their team. You either manage people well or you fail. Discovering your leadership self-image will rescue or prevent a faltering or crumbling career.

In a one day workshop that I often present to companies, I share with them that 86% of successful managers confirm that you cannot lead the cavalry charge if you think you look silly on a horse. Now I know the title of that sounds a little bit silly in itself, but when you take a look at it again and you read it, it's true; you cannot lead the cavalry charge if you think you look silly on a horse.

Being a leadership master takes managers and employees on a journey that will guarantee to give them the self-image that will enable them to lead the cavalry with or without a horse.

Those with a shared goal, also indicated that by sharing their written goal they had to think more about it and how they would achieve it. This resulted in having a plan that they could discuss and use to correct their course in order to achieve their desired outcome.

Remember the whole is always greater than the sum of the parts.

Everything You Need To Learn About Leadership You Can Learn From A P1NEAPPLE

WELCOME TO THE GREAT BY CHOICE
Goal Setting Workbook

Welcome to the Great by Choice Goal Setting Workbook.

Please allow yourself the space and time to complete all the exercises in one sitting. I recommend approximately one hour for completing your Great by Choice Goal Setting Workbook.

You will need a pen and you may need a notebook before you begin. Please ensure you will not be disturbed during the process.

Great by Choice Goal Setting Method in this book is the exact same method I have shared with in my 125 seminars and speeches across a wide spectrum of both business and countries last year.

I have added the Great by Choice Goal Setting Method in this book as a bonus chapter to help you achieve excellence in yourself and those you manage.

I am going to ask a series of question that will form the backbone of you achieving your goals in all areas of your life.

I say all areas of your life because once you have completed the Great by Choice Goal Setting Method workbook you will be able to teach it to your:

- *Colleagues,*
- *Children,*
- *In classes,*
- *In church groups,*
- *You can teach it any where.*

I am going to ask that you complete each question in full before moving onto the next question.

- *There are no trick questions,*
- *There is no wrong answers,*
- *The answers must come from you,*
- *Be honest with yourself,*
- *No one else has to see your answers,*
- *You can be as creative as you can be with your thoughts and answers,*
- *Don't hold back with your creativity for it has the power to become your future.*

Let our journey begin with the first question:

What 5 things have you already accomplished that you are proud of?

The key words here are: what you are proud of, the five things you list can be anything when you achieved them made you feel proud of yourself.

You have accomplished many things in the past let's begin by acknowledging them and giving ourselves credit for them. You can if you choose list more than 5.

The 5 things I am proud of are:

1. _____.
2. _____.
3. _____.
4. _____.
5. _____.

This next question may take a little longer to answer, please take your time and fully answer the question, here is the question:

What do you want in the next 10 years?

Make a list of at least 50 items:

This list is not what you think you can get this list is what you want. If you achieved everything you set out to do in life this list would be a list of all you achieved.

Your list might contain:

- Places you want to visit,
- Be in a film,
- Meet your favourite celebrity,
- Have a baby,

- Become healthier,
- Get promotion,
- Buy a home near the beach,
- Be financially free,
- New hobbies,
- New car,
- Become a great parent,
- Be the next CEO of your company,
- Set a family goal, meaning one that includes all your family.

Please complete the list below:

1. _____
2. _____
3. _____
4. _____
5. _____
6. _____
7. _____
8. _____
9. _____
10. _____

Everything You Need To Learn About Leadership You Can Learn From A P1NEAPPLE

11. _____
12. _____
13. _____
14. _____
15. _____
16. _____
17. _____
18. _____
19. _____
20. _____
21. _____
22. _____
23. _____
24. _____
25. _____
26. _____
27. _____
28. _____
29. _____
30. _____

31. _____
32. _____
33. _____
34. _____
35. _____
36. _____
37. _____
38. _____
39. _____
40. _____
41. _____
42. _____
43. _____
44. _____
45. _____
46. _____
47. _____
48. _____
49. _____
50. _____

Here is the next exercise:

I want you to give each exercise a number, at the side of each item on your list of 50.

The numbers I want you to use are 1, 3, 5, 10 these represent the length of time you realistically think it will take you to achieve you goal.

For example:

If you put on your list to get a degree, which would probably take 3 years to complete. Your list would look something like this:

1. Degree 3

If on your list was to pass your driving test that would take you less than 12 months, you list would now look something like this.

1. Degree 3
2. Pass driving test 1

Go down your list of 50 items and give each one a number that represents the length of time it will take to achieve. Give it your best guesstimate.

Now go through your list and count them. How many ones, how many threes, how many fives, and how many tens?

How many 1's: _____.

How many 3's: _____.

How many 5's: _____.

How many 10's: _____.

If you have set a family goal ensure that all the family celebrate together, it could be a picnic in the park or a walk along the beach.

The second part of this section is that you must also mark it off you list as being achieved.

You can at any time add to your list especially once you have checked one off; again ensuring that you give it a number 1.3. 5. or 10.

This also helps our Reticular Activating System to stay focused on the other goals.

Our goal list needs to be updated and added to on a regular basis, remember if you don't know where you are going any road will take you there and you could end up:

- *Living where you don't want to live,*
- *Driving a car you don't want to drive,*
- *Being with people you don't want to be with.*

One of students started his degree age 72; there are no limits to goal setting:

You cannot have too many:

- *Friends,*
- *Money,*
- *Promotions.*

Here is the next question:

On your list of one year goals which are the 4 most important, go back to you list and pick out the four most important goals.

1. _____.
2. _____.
3. _____.

4. _____.

Don't be the person who is asked when you are going to get going or when are you going to do something with your life.

Live your life with purpose and passion.

As the Ghandi famously said "Be the change you want to see in the world".

Next exercise:

This question is absolutely vital to you, here is the question:

Why are these four goals so important to you?

Let me explain why this is so important:

- *When the why gets stronger the how gets clearer?*
- *When the why gets stronger the how gets easier?*
- *Purpose is stronger than possessions if you wanted be a millionaire the question is why? You see the purpose of becoming a millionaire is to far more rewarding that just having the money in your possession.*
- *There is nothing wrong with having possessions on your list as long as you fully understand the why of having them.*

Try writing out why you want the money it will help you find your why.

If some of your goals are related to you changing you character traits to become for example calmer, less angry then finding your why will be extremely beneficial in your reticular activating system being clearer and more focused on achieving it with you.

It's not what you get that makes you valuable it's what you become that makes you valuable.

Goal 1 is important to me because:

Goal 2 is important to me because:

Goal 3 is important to me because:

Goal 4 is important to me because:

Here is the next exercise:

What type of person must I become in order to achieve all I want?

"What you become helps you to achieve, what you achieve helps you to become"?

"What type of person must I be to 'attract' the people and things that I want in my life?"

"When you knock on the door of opportunity you must have an attractive character or you may not be invited in"?

Start by writing what I must become in order to achieve. Remember the chapter on self-awareness regarding understanding both your strengths and areas you need to develop.

I must become:

_____

_____

_____

Planning:

Take one of your goals and now start the process of planning:

- *What will my goal look and feel like when I have achieved it?*

Write you vision below each question:

How will I know I have achieved my goal, what will it look like?

How will I feel when I achieve it?

_____

_____

How will I appear to the world once I have achieved it?

_____

_____

_____

Will achieving this goal positively affect the people around me? If so how?

_____

_____

- *Do I have the skills needed?*
- *If not where can I acquire them?*
- *Who do I need to mentor me?*

Who do I trust to share my goal with? (You do not have to share all your goals).

Create a goal statement that you can carry around with you and more importantly read it at least twice a day.

A goal statement should contain the following:

› Written in the present tense.

If you goal is to earn a certain amount of money your goal card should read: "I am now earning (insert amount of money)".

› Your goal card should state what you intend to give in return for the money:

"I am now earning (insert amount of money) in return for delivering (insert what you intend to sell, develop, your services).

› The goal card should say when the money will be in your possession.

"I am now earning X £'s in return for delivering X services. The money will come to me in varying amounts before (insert date)".

The card needs to be read every day with passion and enthusiasm.

Clearly define a plan for obtaining your goal:

Remember your brains love:

› Structure,

› Process,

› Plans.

Read your plan every day and at the end of the day ask yourself these three questions:

1. Has my actions today taken me in the direction for me to achieve my goals?

_____

_____

2. Has my actions been positive in relation to my goals?

_____

_____

_____

3. Has my dealing with others been constructive to both parties?

_____

Let's not forget the great lesson from Gold medal winner Lizzy Yarnold. Lizzy won gold in the 2014 winter Olympics in Sochi by hurtling down the ice on a tray at 80 kilometres per hour. Her four runs were faster than her competitors, her first three runs were smoother and with less bumping on the bends than on her forth.

When Lizzy was interviewed a few days after receiving her gold medal she was asked about the fourth run not being as good as the first three; her response was totally inspiring and a great lesson in leadership mastery.

She said:

"You have to remember that no run is ever perfect the trick is to get back on track quicker and faster that everyone else."

"There is no failure only feedback."

The next steps you need to take are to repeat the same exercises for your top four goals from the 3, 5 and 10 year list.

I know this may sound like a lot of work, please remember that without a structure, process and plan your natural default position is chaos.

I shared with you on page 13 the following benefits to reading this book.

There are five major areas that managers, leaders and supervisors will benefit from reading this book or joining The Psychology of Leadership Mastery Mentoring Program.

1. To become the person that company's fight to keep: You have invested a lot of time, effort, and money into your career so far, in this uncertain economic time. "Everything you ever needed to learn about leadership you can learn from a pineapple!" will help you get the best return on your investment in you. Getting the best is far more rewarding than getting the most out of people.

2. Establishing a rewarding career does not always mean a higher salary, it may mean you acquire the prestige, status, and influence that will carry you through all areas of your life.

3. Become the person people look up to, no matter how tall they grow! Learn how to form and maintain lasting relationships in work and in your personal life that are built on Trust and Respect.

4. Become the best you can be and be the master of your own destiny. Experience the challenge of opening up new areas of your life and feel the excitement of practicing new skills that will help you get the best out of life.

5. All human beings have a built in desire to be emotionally connected with life. We need to feel alive and have meaning and purpose in our lives. We do not have time for boredom and mindless repetition.

These points were not shared just for fun they are directly linked to the five hard wired drives in the brain.

These statements have been designed to trigger with in people one or more of those five drives.

You are designed for greatness and engineered for success.

Please don't waste that greatness; it takes persistence and a plan to be a success in any area of life.

Persistence is the key to implementing you plan, every day you should have taken action that moves you closer to the goal you have set.

Every day you should have read your goal card.

Every day you should be visualising your desired goal as being achieved.

As a leader manager or supervisor please keep as your mantra:

Are my actions positive, constructive and taking US in the direction WE want to go in?

If not change course immediately because there is no failure only feedback.

If I can help in any way in implementing the Great by Choice Goal Setting Program or the Leadership Mastery Mentoring Program please contact me on: 01224 548 814.

Or email me at: john@leadershipmastery.co.uk

One Final Thought

I started this book by sharing with you the following questions that have been the focus of my twenty-five year research into the psychology of leadership mastery. Here are the three questions;

1. What takes a person from average to outstanding?

2. What are the differences between an outstanding performer and an average one?

3. And more importantly, to help us answer, why people know what to do, so why the hell don't they do it?

When you begin to integrate the information contained in this book into your daily life both at work and at home you will started your journey from where you are now to outstanding.

You have the information to begin the journey you now need to use it; to put into daily practice in order to fully understand the power each piece of information has in being the difference that makes the difference.

Implementing the tried, tested and proven techniques will help eliminate; 'Why People Know What To Do, So Why The Hell Don't They Do It.'

I know that if you will start this journey you will enjoy more success more often and more easily with less stress less hassle and less frustration.

I hope you have enjoyed learning lessons from the pineapple and as I said in my first book: *'Great Leaders Never Climb Smooth Mountains: How To Avoid The 17 1/2 Routes To Ineffective Leadership.'* Sometimes the climb is not smooth but then again nobody ever climbed a smooth mountain.

John at the top of Hellvellyn.
"Nobody ever climbed a smooth mountain"

Enjoy the journey if you feel I could help you in any way please give me a call or email me, my promise to you is this; there will be no hard sell or pressure, just two professional discussing how we can help each other to add value.

For further information about applying the information contained in this book:

✓ In specific situations, such as;

✓ Working with a manager being groomed for promotion.

✓ Mentoring high performing executives whose personality styles impacts negatively on their relationship with peers, staff and clients.

✓ Working with executives wishing to develop their career paths and prospects.

✓ Mentoring as a follow up from EQ / 360-degree performance appraisals.

✓ Increasing the executives psychological and personal mastery skills such as self-awareness, recognition of personal 'blind spots', defences and limiting thoughts, beliefs and emotional effectiveness.

✓ Improving the balance between work and life demands.

✓ Improving the executive's leadership, management and team building skills.

✓ Mentoring an executive to work more effectively within a changing organisational structure.

✓ Working with a leader to coach others in transition.

✓ Communication skills.

✓ Performance management appraisals.

✓ Helping the individual executive who requires new skills for a new position due to change in organisational structure.

✓ Developing Confidence And Self Esteem.

Please contact JOHN EDINGTON 'The Pineapple Man' to discover more about the varying programmes offered under the umbrella of:

www.leadershipmastery.co.uk

Email: john@leadershipmastery.co.uk

Telephone. 01224 548 814

JOHN EDINGTON

Author, Keynote Speaker and Broadcaster in Leadership Mastery.

<u>Books and Training Programmes</u>

<u>by John Keith Edington</u>

"Great Leaders Never Climb Smooth Mountains' How to avoid the 17½ routes to ineffective leadership"

"People know what to do so why the 'HELL' don't they do it?"

"You cannot lead the cavalry charge if you think you look silly on a horse" Developing a leadership mindset.

"Everything You Ever Needed To Learn About Leadership You Can Learn From A Pineapple"

"People Know What To Do So Why The 'HELL' Don't They Do It?"

I am repeatedly asked by senior executives, CEO's and HR professionals:

"People know what to do, so why the 'Hell' don't they do it?"

This is just one of the three frequently asked questions, the other two I will also share with you later. Based on my work with hundreds of companies, I have noticed that managers and leaders consistently struggle with this question.

Discover what 1,233 of the world's most successful business leaders have learned, applied and attributed to their success. You will learn the essential, tried, tested and proven leadership skills and techniques needed to become a highly effective leader in any business.

"You Cannot Lead The Cavalry Charge If You Think You Look Silly On A Horse"

Based on the research by fellow Psychologist and leading neuroscientists of how the brain records and communicates in picture because;

"We Cannot Consistently Out Perform The Image We Have Of Ourselves"

This interactive workshop will show you how to change both your thinking and the image you have of yourself; therefore creating excellence within your business.

It is designed to assist businesses with their greatest asset, People.

Leaders are continually mentoring and developing their personnel and those they lead in order to; Create Excellence Within People, understanding the how to and why to help people change is the foundation stone for building a successful leadership career.

John is also known as the Pineapple guy! For his humorous delivery and book,

"Everything You Ever Needed To Learn About Leadership You Can Learn From A Pineapple"

A light hearted and poignant look at leadership taught to us from the versatility and king of fruit; the pineapple.

Discover the10 most rewarding connections that the king of fruit has to offer those on the leadership path.

The Pineapple is not, strictly speaking, one fruit. Rather it is 100-200 fruitlets all fused together around the core, what a great metaphor for a modern day leader who needs to fuse his team around the core of the business.

Leadership is transferring ideas to the minds of others, the clearer you transfer those ideas the more rewarding your career or business will be.

"The Roots And Wings Of Raising Positive Kids In A Negative World"

One of my passions in life is helping children to grow into health emotionally functioning adults, while helping their parents to give their children both roots and wings.

To only dream of the person you could be is to waste the person you are.

"As a parent I have been given hundreds of articles to read concerning parenting, this book is the first that has not left me feeling guilty.

The book is a positive aid to parenting; it is amazing I feel it is the best advice on parenting I have ever experienced. It was no effort to read and understand. I found the whole experience extremely helpful" -LL.

JOHN EDINGTON

John at the top of Hellvellyn.
"Nobody ever climbed a smooth mountain"

Award winning motivational speaker and presenter John speaks with authority, clarity and humour.

He is also known as the Pineapple Man!

He has a gifted ability to translate leading achievement psychological research into effortless, coherent, compelling and exciting knowledge that is instantly actionable.

His knowledge is not purely academic.

He has owned and run several highly successful businesses, taking one of his businesses to a 6458% increase in turnover.

John has worked extensively across the UK, Europe and Australia which has made him one of the leading speakers and most powerful professional mentor to heads of businesses, Olympic athletes and leading professionals.

Last year John conducted more than 125 seminars and speeches across a wide spectrum of both business and countries.

When he is not working, John lives with his wife in the Yorkshire Dales where his passion for his hobbies of walking and escaping to the Northumberland coast in his motor home are more than catered for.

"IT IS KNOWING HOW TO BE DIFFERENT THAT MAKES THE DIFFERENCE"

*A Vision without action is a daydream.
Action without vision is a nightmare.*
Japanese Proverb

I am so confident that I can help ignite your bottom line profit I am offering you a free lunch and learn session, lasting 58 minutes, where I will show you and your senior management team how to create excellence in themselves and those they manage.

I am offering this to you because we don't yet know each other and this way you get to see just how I can help your business with no risk or cost (other than the cost of the lunch and possibly a hotel room depending on the distance) to you. 100% guaranteed.

My promise to you is this; there will be no hard sell or pressure, i want our relationship to be built on honesty, trust and mutual respect.

If you would like a free down loadable version of my first book:

"Great Leaders Never Climb Smooth Mountains' How to avoid the 17½ routes to ineffective leadership"

Or a free downloadable copy of:

"People know what to do so why the 'HELL' don't they do it?"

Please email me @ john@leadershipmastery.co.uk

Or through the website www.thepineappleman.co.uk

Add in optical reader here and on back page.

Are Your Employees The Most Complex Creatures on the Planet?

There are some employees who can sit for hours during the working day and be entertained by absolutely nothing and there are those employees who will consistently give 100% effort and commitment every day.

I just think it's fascinating how creatures so wondrously made as we are can be so single minded. Take the likeness of a Rubik cube; do you know the estimated number of permutations to complete the Rubik cube?

The answer is 43 billion, billion.

The minimum number of permutations is 20!

Getting the best from each employee is a simple process that can either take 20 moves or anywhere up to 43 billion, billion moves.

Make your first move now by giving me a call or email me for a no obligation chat on;

www.leadershipmastery.co.uk

Email: john@leadershipmastery.co.uk

Telephone. 01224 548 814

www.ingramcontent.com/pod-product-compliance
Lightning Source LLC
Chambersburg PA
CBHW060853170526
45158CB00001B/332